AMBUSHED BY CANCER

THE CAREGIVER TELLS HER STORY

Helen Bartucca

First Edition

NEWMAN SPRINGS PUBLISHING
320 Broad Street
Red Bank, NJ 07701

First originally published by Newman Springs Publishing 2023

ISBN 978-1-68498-641-5 (Paperback)
ISBN 978-1-68498-642-2 (Digital)

Printed in the United States of America

To Dr. Eric Jacobsen, MD, Dana-
Farber Cancer Institute.

We, as caregivers, might never be recognized for our contribution, but without a doubt, we will have made one person's life journey a better one.

—B. Joyce Gilmore, RN (Retd.)[1]

CONTENTS

PART 3: TAPS AND STEADY FOOTING

PREFACE

As Frank's wife, caregiver, and best friend, I navigated the light and dark of cancer with him. He did not talk much about what he was going through; he did not need to for my benefit, I could see, and though I ached to help him feel better, I could not.

At the time of Frank's diagnosis, I knew no one who was, or had been, a caregiver for a person with such a serious illness. At first, I felt confident we would walk together to conquer the cancer and continue our travels across the United States. I didn't anticipate that as time went on, Frank would often withdraw into himself, simply to survive another day. I worried that I might not have the stamina to care for Frank and manage the household on my own. If I shared these fears with family and friends, they might see me as incompetent or weak-spirited. I was loath to be seen that way, as much as I was loath to force others to feel obligated to take over my responsibilities, regardless of their willingness.

When I opened up to my primary care physician about these fears, she faced me squarely, held my hands, and said, "You need to talk with someone who has gone through this and had a successful outcome." I wasn't sure how that would help. I would rather have talked with someone who was going through what I was right at that moment so we could say to each other, "Yeah, I feel the same," or "It's okay," or "How long do you think these feelings will last?"

The only time I came close to finding that person was at the elevator in the stem cell-transplant wing of Frank's hospital. She was a stranger waiting for the doors to open. We looked at each other long enough for us to smile that knowing smile. I asked if her husband was going through stem cell transplant. She said he was, but he was not doing well. We did not need to say more. Our hands touched briefly, the elevator doors opened, and she was gone.

For those of us who are older, whose body parts and organs already complain and sometimes quit, we can only hope there is reserve and strength enough for us to be caregivers and reserve enough for the patients to endure the onslaught of grueling treatments. The lot of the caregiver is a tough one and one for which most of us have little to no training. It forces us to learn quickly and react smartly. It requires us to be vigilant, diligent, and compassionate, while often not knowing the outcome.

PART 1

SLIPPING IN SHADOWS

2014

Time sometimes flies like a bird,
sometimes crawls like a snail; but a man
is happiest when he does not even notice
whether it passes swiftly or slowly.

—Ivan Turgenev, Russian author (1818–1883)[2]

CHAPTER 1

Uncle Vanya and the Shadowed Grape

It is opening night of *Uncle Vanya*, April 2014, in a small community theater in Central Massachusetts. I eye the empty seat in the very last row next to the wall, but before I start sidestepping in front of others seated in that row, I am surprised when an usher gently takes my elbow and pulls me back toward the aisle.

"There are seats in the front row," he says with a youthful smile while still pulling on my elbow.

I pull away and tell him I'll take the last seat in the back row. He ignores me and whispers that I will be able to hear better up front, as though this is a secret between us; he is the young man, and I am the old lady.

"No, thank you," I say and make my way past the knees of those already seated in the back row.

My hearing is fine. What's not fine is that my attention span is very short for plays that do not grab me in the first few minutes. I will become groggy and am apt to fall asleep, hoping I don't snore, or worse, that I get tapped on the shoulder by a neighbor telling me to shush, which has happened more than once.

Lobby lights blink, the house lights begin to fade, someone coughs that final cough, and a hush settles in the theater. I scrunch my winter coat into a fine pillow that will rest between my shoulder and the wall, ready if needed. All is quiet as the spotlight comes up on an old man, bent forward from the waist, taking slow deliberate steps across the stage, as though trying not to stumble. His gray hair is scraggly on the back of his neck, his beard rough and clearly unshaven for weeks, and his eyebrows are bushy and long over his eyes. This is my husband, Frank, who stands over six feet tall offstage, is lean and strong, with thick black hair and matching mustache that are always trim and neat. Onstage tonight, there is no hint of his straight back or broad shoulders, only an old man tottering across the stage. His deep voice rises to where I am sitting.

I take a long breath and nudge the wall with my shoulder. I have heard his lines so often at home that, if needed, I could whisper a cue. Seconds before I start to relax, however, I notice something on the right side of Frank's neck. It looks like a lump, the size of a half grape. As I lean forward, my coat falls to the floor, and I leave it there. The swelling is right above his costume collar, and in the bright stage lighting, it is large enough to cast a shadow. When other actors enter the stage, Frank turns, and for most of the first act, I cannot see the right side of his neck. I wonder how long it has been there, unnoticed by either of us, too large to have appeared this evening. Had Frank known about it, he would have mentioned it. The play unfolds, more actors enter the stage, and each time I see the shadowed lump, I am alarmed it may be something serious. After the actors' final bows, I gather up my coat and walk to the lobby to greet Frank.

Only a few years back, Frank came home downcast after his very first audition for a role with a local community theater. Had I known his interest in theater was serious, I might not have shrugged off his hours of moodiness and instead offered encouragement, but he never spoke of wanting to be part of theater. When I finally pressed him, he looked at me with raised eyebrows and confessed that he had broken character and lost his place and voice. I stifled a chuckle, thinking it couldn't be that serious, but it was that serious to Frank, and I was taken aback, unsure how his love of theater escaped me.

"You know, there just aren't many roles for older men, and I blew it!"

Age takes its toll on more than our bodies, and right now, I knew Frank felt cheated, that he had started this dream too late.

Now after years of classes and hard work, he has gathered a following in the local theater community and has his own successful theater company, 4th Wall Stage Company, where he can choose the plays he wants to direct and choose the parts he wants to play. I give myself credit for naming his theater company 4th Wall, that invisible wall between the audience and actors, that wall he yearns to stand behind.

Tonight I lean against the lobby wall and watch longtime admirers shake his hand while telling him how they love watching him perform. I marvel at how calm he is with all the attention.

Not me; unlike Frank, I am happiest in the background, observing. Looking back, the closest I came to acting was years before I met Frank, when I lived in a small New Hampshire town. On a warm spring night, I walked through the town's central park, canopied by elm and maple trees, to the town hall. I opened the heavy wooden doors and climbed the red-carpeted stairs to the theater for the first night of auditions for the musical *Annie Get Your Gun*. I tiptoed down the aisle in the darkened theater, feeling much like an intruder. Under the lights on the stage, a man stood to the side making notes and barking out orders, "Louder, please," or "You're not made of wood, move your arms, walk, lean into the role!" I sat in a middle row, halfway back, as risk-free as I could get. By the end of the auditions, even I could tell who had "it" and who didn't.

"Hey, we need someone to walk on stilts," the director shouted, just as I rose from my seat to leave. Pause.

"Anyone?" he shouted.

For the longest time, no one responded, and by now the stage was nearly empty. Since I could walk on stilts, I raised my hand and shouted back that I could. I was sure I still could. As kids, we would have races on our stilts, giggle when we lost balance, hop back up, and continue the race.

"Okay," he said. "What's your name?"

"Helen."

"Stand so I can see you," he said, shielding his eyes from the lights.

He turned away from me, shuffled papers on a stand in front of him, and instructed, "Tuesday, show up for the first rehearsal."

"You'll have the stilts, right?" I shouted back, thinking they would be simple poles reaching to my armpits with small platforms for my feet, the kind we used as kids.

"No, you need to bring your own, and make sure you are three feet above the ground and that your hands are free. You have to walk across the stage and onto a platform that juts into the audience to throw confetti." He made a quick motion with his arm as though throwing confetti far into the audience.

"And make sure you can do it alone! I'm relying on you. It's a short role but an important one." With that, he packed up and left.

Oh god! I barely slept that night.

The next morning, I sat behind my desk at work, where my corner office had large windows overlooking the park. My job as executive director of Community Development was a lucky one at that time. My two coworkers were rehabilitation specialists who oversaw the construction on substandard apartments and homes. Had it not been for their intimate knowledge of stilts, I most likely never would have walked across that stage.

"There's no problem here," they said. "All you need are stilts three feet off the ground. We'll have them for you by Monday, in time for your Tuesday rehearsal."

Then the phones started ringing, and the workday began.

The following Monday morning, five days after the auditions, the stilts were delivered to my office. I looked them over.

"Sheet Rockers' stilts." My coworkers smiled. "That's how they reach ceilings without a ladder."

As they pointed to the leather straps screwed to the platforms, they instructed, "You'll need to strap your feet in good and tight."

For me, it would be like clamping ski boots onto skis; that part was easy. What was not easy was imagining myself three feet above the ground with nothing to hold on to, knowing that if I fell, I could not free myself. For the next five weeks at lunchtime, these coworkers walked alongside me in the park, allowing me to touch their heads, first with my palms, then with the tips of a finger for support when I got tippy. Cars stopped and passersby laughed, but I kept my concentration.

On opening night backstage, I rolled up the cuffs of my costume pants, sat on a five-foot-high cement shelf, strapped my feet into the bindings, and lowered the extra three feet of pant legs so the stilts were invisible. When it came time to walk onto the platform that jutted into the audience, I was ready: shoulders squared, balance sure. As I threw confetti onto heads right down there in front me, I could see their eyes looking up at me and knew they were holding their breaths, pleading I didn't end up on their laps. I was hardly prepared for the round of applause when I returned to the stage, but I felt it radiate inside me, like sprinkles of sugar bouncing off my ribs, giving me a zinging rush inside.

That was my last time onstage. Frank and I are so different; he loves all that theater involves: producing, directing, acting. My interests are in music and painting. He will look forward to memorizing pages of lines, not only his but the lines of other actors as well, in case a line is skipped or forgotten; I can barely memorize two measures of music. His play choices are dramas, always with subtleties I often don't understand. My play choices are musicals, light and, better yet, comical.

On the hour-long trip home from the theater this April evening, Frank and I both concentrate on the highway and its faded lane lines as we move through the rain and feel the vibration of speeding tractor trailers as they pass. I say nothing about the swelling. A better time will be later, when we settle before a nice fire, when Frank has his martini, I have my wine, and the excitement of the performance wanes. As we turn into our long driveway, and the headlights catch the garage and breezeway leading to the house, I am glad to be safely home, away from heavy trucks and the dark of this rain-slicked night. When we walk into the house, all is quiet until Persy, our nine-pound Yorkshire terrier, bursts with excitement, runs around the room, and stops only for a quick pat before running to the kitchen, where she skids across the tiled floor. It is a well-rehearsed greeting, the same every time we come home.

Finally we sit on the sofa with Persy asleep between our legs. We listen to the spit and crackle of the fire.

"When you first entered the stage walking as an old man, which, by the way, you did so well, I barely recognized you." Frank is smiling, and I wait, then say, "I saw a swelling, a lump, on your neck."

"A lump?" He turns to look at me, his brow furrows, and puts down his glass to feel his neck, but he cannot find it.

"On the right side." I hold his fingers to direct them to the spot.

"Here?" he asks, probing with his fingertips. "Ah, I feel it." His voice is even, with no sense of alarm, which eases my anxiety. "What do you suppose that is?" he asks.

"I don't know. Does it hurt?"

"No. Wonder how long that's been there."

"You should have it looked at."

Both our hands rest on Persy, still snuggled between us. We sit quietly for some time, and our conversation returns to tomorrow night's performance, which will play to another full house.

Later that evening, before bed, Frank stands at the bathroom mirror checking his neck. "I have to work around the rest of this play and photography classes to see the doctor. We have nine more performances, and the photography assignments can't be put aside," he says.

I don't agree. Had the lump been on my neck, I would be planning to call the doctor the first thing next morning and would be willing to forego anything on my calendar, but Frank is not like that. He will methodically work through the timing of assignments, check his calendar, then call the doctor. There is no point in my asking him to speed it up.

We do not discuss it further that night, and during the next few days, our routines take over. But during a dental cleaning, the hygienist finds another lump on his neck and tells him it should be checked by his doctor. If Frank is concerned about this second swelling, possibly on his thyroid, he does not show it this time either. In passing, he tells me his appointment with his primary care physician is in a few days. He is happy to get on with photography assignments at Boston University, where he is enrolled in the photography program in the Center for Digital Arts. He is also busy working out the details for his next two plays, which open in September of this year and February of next year.

Meanwhile, I am uneasy about something too vague to label. I tell myself that thinking it might be cancer seems unreasonable and melodramatic. If I mention this to Frank, he will scowl and remind me I am overreacting and tell me to wait until we have something to worry about. Still, I'm concerned.

The morning Frank leaves for the appointment with his primary care physician, I am outside in the warmth of the May sun, pulling weeds, planting pansies, and readying the ground for annuals around the swimming pool. In one month, when the temperature warms, splashes of color will transform the browns and grays of winter to yellows and bright oranges and reds, and the flowers will give off the sweet smells of spring. Persy sticks close by as I kneel to plant the flowers, pushing her bright-yellow beach ball into my hands. When I nudge it away, she pushes it back. I laugh at this game we always play when I'm busy in the gardens, until finally I throw it and watch as she bounces it off her nose from one side of the yard to the other, like a seal in a circus act. When Frank's car stops in the garage, I wash my hands and meet him in the house.

"The doctor has ordered biopsies on my thyroid and one of the lumps on my neck," he says.

"Lumps. More than one?" This I didn't expect.

"He felt two more today on my neck." Frank walks to the kitchen counter and takes a handful of pistachio nuts. He does not seem alarmed.

"I have to have a CT scan," he says matter-of-factly. "I don't know what he is looking for, but I am not going to worry until I have something to worry about."

"Me too," I lie and leave the kitchen to return to my gardening and Persy and her bright-yellow ball.

A few days later, I sit in the day surgery waiting room, trying to knit or read, but I find it difficult to concentrate. After an hour or so, Frank returns with a bandage on the side of his neck and a bandage under his chin. In a week, he will have the CT scan. Shortly after that, his primary care doctor will have the results.

Meanwhile, the days pass easily until Frank arrives home with the biopsy results. The porch door is open, letting in fresh spring air with the smell of lilacs. When his car door closes, Persy rushes to the screen door, jumps like a kangaroo on her hind legs, and, when Frank walks in, runs in circles around the room until finally leaping onto his lap, licking his chin.

"The hero's welcome no matter what!" He laughs. "It's a good thing she only weighs nine pounds."

I sit on the sofa and wait for the news.

"Some is good," he says. "The tissue removed during surgery on my thyroid is benign."

He grins, but his eyes tell something else. I watch him take a deep breath as I hold mine.

"The tissue from the lymph node, under my chin, is non-Hodgkin follicular lymphoma."

"What is that?"

"Cancer." He raises his eyebrows, shrugs his shoulders, and adds, "I've an appointment with an oncologist Monday."

"Do you have any more information?"

"That's all I know right now."

"What about the CT scan results?"

"We'll get those when I see the oncologist on Monday."

Persy snuggles under his chin. I watch Frank's hands gently rub her tiny ears and wonder what he might be thinking. His face is calm.

"I feel fine," he says.

"I'm going with you to the oncologist."

We do not say much after that. We will wait until Monday, three days away, to learn more.

Persy and I go outside. I throw her ball a couple times and wonder how such a small ball of fur can run that fast while bouncing a ball on her nose. My stomach is knotting with worry. I feel a darkness in me, this fear that the cancer is serious and may somehow impact our lives. When I look in a mirror, I see the start of creases between my eyebrows, my lips pulled in between my teeth, watery eyes, and stiffened shoulders. I cannot escape this anxiety.

I call my daughters, Jeannie and Lynne, who live minutes away, and my son, who lives in Alaska. They are my strongest supporters. I hear a silence and the intake of breath as they try to figure out what to say to me. I want to help them, but I have no words either.

Jeannie and Lynne say the same thing in the same hushed voice, "Do you want me to come over? How is Frank taking this? We love you both."

"No need to come over. I just needed to share this, maybe dilute some of the sting."

My next calls are to my brothers, who also live in Massachusetts, a couple of hours away. Their response is the same hushed quiet.

Frank has been estranged from his son and daughter for years but has kept in close contact with his brother, his only other relative. He asks that we not share this diagnosis with friends until we know more.

There is no creature whose inward being is so strong that it is not greatly determined by what lies outside it.

—George Eliot
(Marion Evans Cross) 1819–1880[3]

CHAPTER 2

The Long Corridor

May 2014

We hold hands and silently walk down the long corridor of the hematology/oncology wing of the hospital for our first appointment with the oncologist. Frank looks healthy and feels fine. People must look at us and think we do not belong here. The corridor is bright, with sunshine filtering in through tall windows on our right. They overlook a large grassy area near the parking lot, an island of respite in an otherwise busy network of roads and parking garages. I wonder if benches and tables will appear later this spring for people to enjoy the sun and fresh air. If I have hours to wait for Frank while he is having some procedure, I can see myself sitting there, away from reminders of cancer. The left side of this corridor is a gray wall with pictures of muted splats of color framed and hung at eye level. They seem tasteless, mass-produced, and institutional, as though the buyer hurriedly walked the aisles of a chain store pointing a finger and saying, "Oh, I'll take this one, and that one," unaware that pictures can create feelings of calm. If we are lucky, the right pictures will make us stop to look and perhaps become part of the picture, if only for a brief moment, and what a gift that would be for those walking this corridor.

At the check-in desk, Frank shows his insurance and ID cards and receives a patient ID bracelet. The waiting area is divided into two parts. We are told to sit on one side first and wait to be called for blood work. We don't find two chairs together, and no one offers to move, so we sit in the corridor on a bench by the tall glass window where we can be together. I feel myself holding my breath, so I relax my shoulders and make myself take in a long slow breath while I count to four, hold it as I count to two, and let it out to the count of four. That works for a few tries until I watch a man walk slowly by us who looks so much like Frank's character in *Uncle Vanya*, with scraggly gray hair falling around his collar and his body hunched, that I am taken aback. This old man is leaning heavily on the handles of a wheelchair, his body so slumped I think he might topple if he let go. His feet shuffle. The woman in the wheelchair smiles at me; I smile back. Her face is very wrinkled, her head is wrapped in a colorful scarf, a plush baby-blue fleece blanket covers her lap. The man must have left his car with valet parking, I think, because he seems too frail to have navigated the parking garage, the elevator, and this long corridor on his way to the check-in desk.

No age is immune. Some patients are young enough to have small children. A young woman in her twenties with a scarf covering her head and a white bracelet around her pencil-thin wrist sits crossed-legged, fiddling with the bracelet, her eyes blinking as though irritated by a speck of dust. One man in his forties, dressed for work in a coat and tie, sits across from us with a leather briefcase by his feet. Some are in their midseventies, like Frank and me. Many are gray-haired and very wrinkled. Sitting quietly two chairs away from us is another gray-haired man, probably the same age as we are, with no bracelet on his wrist. Perhaps he is waiting for a cancer patient to return from blood work.

Looking at the patients and their companions, breathing this same air, hearing the same sounds, I begin to imagine what I may be facing. I have no reason to think Frank will have pencil-thin wrists; he is too heavy-boned for that, but I know cancer patients lose weight and hair and that nausea is a big problem. I tell myself Frank will continue theater, photography, and golf, and I will continue playing cornet in my band, taking watercolor classes, and spending time with my grandchildren. There have been times in my life when holding onto good positive thoughts was an effort, and I seem to be right back there now, but those times were before I met Frank. They eventually faded, replaced by happier times that have lasted.

With my back against the large window overlooking the expanse of green, I straighten my shoulders and work on my breathing again but find it too difficult to concentrate. Cancer patients die, and I am frightened for Frank and myself. It's not only the cancer and possible death; it's the financial strain. I know we have insurance that will help us weather some of this, but I'm not sure how much it will cover. I shudder to think our savings may be wiped out and what that would mean for us. Certainly we are more fortunate than many families who have little or no insurance. I can't bear to think of their struggle, especially if they have children. I feel a cascading fear and have to stop thinking about this now. I do not know what to expect from this appointment.

Finally Frank is called in for blood work. I wait alone on the bench, trying not to stare at the others seated here, and wonder what they are going through. It is quiet except for the *tap-tap* of the receptionist's fingers on a computer keyboard.

Frank returns; his brow is knitted.

"Took her forever to find the right spot to stick the needle," he complains.

We move to the other waiting room, wait to be called to see the oncologist, and try to play a mindless game on the computer, but neither of us can concentrate, so we wait. We are newcomers to this oncology floor, but I can tell many are not by the books, knitting, and computers they have at their side; they know what to expect and are prepared to wait. They do not speak or smile or look up; we all seem huddled in our thoughts.

Today we get the CT scan results. Frank's name is called for the second time, and we enter the doctor's office, where we sit quietly in two chairs and wait. There is a faint knock on the door. Dr. A. greets us with a smile and a handshake. He is middle-aged and a bit pudgy, with thick black hair, not much taller than I am. He is wearing a white lab coat, a distinct status reminder that he is the educated oncologist, and we are the patient and spouse. He asks Frank how he is feeling and then asks him to remove his shirt. I watch as his fingertips rub over Frank's neck, under his arms, and around his belly. He has a pleasant smile, and after the examination, he talks to us, making eye contact, but I have to ask him to speak up because unless he raises his voice, Frank will not hear every word.

Recently Frank's hearing has worsened. He often asks me to repeat something, but there are times when I know he has not heard me at all, and I have to stand close and face him when I speak. Considering the artillery, mortar shells, the roar of jet engines, and hours in helicopters and cargo planes in Vietnam, it is not surprising his hearing suffers, and though we have talked about hearing aids, Frank is aware of the stigma they carry and feels his hearing is adequate now. Had I pushed for them, he would have pushed back.

Dr. A. explains that non-Hodgkin follicular lymphoma is a fairly common cancer. It occurs in the lymph nodes, and unfortunately, it cannot be cured; Frank will always have it. It has four stages. From the CT scan, we know Frank's cancer is stage 3, which means the cancerous lymph nodes are above and below his diaphragm, and the cancer has not spread to nearby organs. Until Frank has a bone marrow biopsy, we won't know if it has progressed to his bone, which would be stage 4. There is no cure, Dr. A. repeats, and unless Frank has symptoms, there is no treatment. He raises his eyebrows and smiles, and I wonder if this might be the course it takes with Frank: no symptoms, no treatment, no slowing down, and life resumes.

"What are the symptoms?" Frank asks as he tucks in his shirt and fastens his belt.

Dr. A. lists them: soaking night sweats requiring a change of sheets, considerable loss of appetite, fatigue, and pain. They seem easy to identify. Soaking night sweats? Of course I'll know that, and change the sheets. Loss of appetite? Sure, we eat most our meals together, and if Frank picks at his food, then I'll know. Fatigue? I suppose if after a good night's sleep and midafternoon nap, he's tired, that should be easy to spot. Pain? I hope not, but I will know.

Dr. A. tells us that should symptoms appear, chemotherapy is required to slow the growth of the cancer. As he lists the types of chemicals for chemotherapy, sometimes referring to them as cocktails, my mind glazes over these words; I've not heard them before. In addition to the symptoms listed, the cancer may also transform into another type of cancer, but he doesn't tell us what kind. I don't think to ask, but I wonder if there would be symptoms that would alert us to this? Right then, Dr. A. turns to his computer, taps a few keys, and tells us that what we are seeing on the screen is a picture from Frank's CT scan. Near the top and at the bottom of the screen, the area above and below Frank's diaphragm, are a series of highlighted spots that look like harmless pearls to me, but they are the cancerous lymph nodes. I look at Frank and try to imagine those spots inside him, but it is hard because he looks healthy and has the same energy and strength he has had for years.

Frank and I look at each other as we try to absorb this.

We are assured the protocol is correct, and that chemotherapy would start only when there are symptoms. The survival rate after chemotherapy is fairly high compared to the survival rate of other cancers. He has a reassuring smile and adds that blood work will continue every three months, and he will order a bone marrow biopsy. When he asks if we have any more questions, we both shake our heads. We gather up our belongings, shake his hand, and leave. Because the path of this cancer is a mystery, and we are to stand by and wait, there is nothing for us to do except show up for the biopsy. If the results are favorable, we continue our day-to-day routine.

On the way home, we stop for pizza. When the waitress asks how we are, I tell her we just left the hospital with news that was not very good. She pulls back her shoulders, and she says she is sorry, and with that I wonder just how open to be with strangers. It's hard to watch an eager smile change quickly to a frown, that expression of sad concern. At home, I phone family with news that no treatment is recommended right now unless the bone marrow biopsy tells us otherwise. Frank calls his brother.

A week later, we have good news from the bone marrow biopsy: the lymphoma in Frank's bone marrow is in such small trace amounts that the diagnosis is still stage 3 non-Hodgkin follicular lymphoma, and since he has no symptoms, there is still no treatment recommended, and blood work will be taken again in three months

I always wonder why birds choose to stay in the same place when they can fly anywhere on the earth. Then I ask myself the same question.

—Harun Yahya[4]

CHAPTER 3

Not by Car!

Summer and Fall 2014

It is midsummer now. Frank feels fine and continues theater and photography. We are back in our routine. If his energy holds, and he continues to have no symptoms, he will not tell his golf group he has cancer and worry them. As for me, I am happy to fill the warm summer days with my four young granddaughters, who arrive nearly every day to swim, do crafts, and run with Persy as she bounces her yellow beach ball on her nose like a seal. On a few summer evenings, I join the trumpet section of a band when we play for the residents of nursing homes. I sense the shadow of cancer slipping far away, and it feels good. These are my happiest days, filled with music, watermelon, and laughter.

On a hot sunny day, Lynne and Jeannie arrive to pick up their girls, but there is something unsettling on Lynne's face.

"What's going on?" I ask.

"We are moving."

"What!" Jeannie all but shouts. "Are you kidding? You just got here."

"It's been six years," Lynne struggles to say. "I'm sorry."

"Well, that's not long enough," Jeannie says abruptly. "I know you promised to stay for these six years so the kids would get to know their cousins"—long pause—"and they did, but—"

I put my hand on Lynne's shoulder. "Where are you going?"

"Seattle. It's a new job."

"What! That's over three thousand miles away."

"I know. I'm sorry."

I ask if the girls know. "Not yet."

With her arms outstretched, Lynne moves close to hug us. Jeannie is the first to wipe a tear. I'm not surprised.

"When are you leaving?" I ask.

"As soon as the house is sold. It's going on the market next week."

"That's quick," is all I can think to say at the moment. As the conversation moves to the logistics of their moving and traveling across the country, I am balancing wishing them well and dreading their leaving. I leave Jeannie and Lynne to their conversation and dip my hands in the pool.

"Come for dinner tonight," I say. "We'll celebrate the new job, your move, all that lies ahead, and give you a good send-off."

As they leave the driveway, the girls shout, "Can we bring our bathing suits?"

"Of course. I'll swim with you," I shout back, listening to peals of laughter trail behind their car like bubbles in the wind. Persy stands beside me. Her ball is nowhere in sight. We both seem deflated.

Three years ago in the late spring, while gardening in the backyard, I felt the hair prickle on the back of my neck and knew that something wasn't right. I looked up to see a strange man standing on our breezeway about ten feet from me, hands on hips, his chest rising and falling, dressed in dirty jeans, stained T-shirt, and hair in a ponytail, quiet, just staring at me. I didn't know how long he had been there.

"What do you want?" I asked, standing up from my weeding at the edge of the pool. He said nothing as he took a step toward me. "I'll get my husband," I said firmly and walked straight into the house through a side door, locked all the doors, and prayed Frank would come home soon. Through the front window, I watched the man's pickup back down the driveway, leaving black tire marks, and heard the squeal of tires on the country road as he sped away. My view was blocked by the overhanging elm and maple trees lining the driveway, and I never got the make or license number.

Later, when Frank came home, I told him, "I need something to tell me someone is here. The driveway is long, and when I'm out back, I can't hear a car. That man scared me, and what would have happened if the kids were here?"

"I'm usually here," Frank said matter-of-factly. He is 6'2", and I'm 5'4"; we look at the world differently.

"Yes, but not always."

"What do you want to do?"

"I want to get a dog that will bark to warn me."

"A dog! No, I know nothing about dogs."

"That's okay. I do."

"No. They shed."

"We'll get one that doesn't shed."

"They're big and awkward to be around."

"We'll get a small one."

"One that yips all the time?"

"We'll train it."

"Who will train it? I don't know a thing about dogs. They slobber. Please, I don't want a dog."

"Well, not all dogs slobber." I watched his shoulders drop, his eyes watching me, but I didn't give in. "Okay," I said calmly. "I will see what dog is small, doesn't shed or slobber, and if we find one, I'll sign up for training lessons." Then I waited through the long sighs and pursed lips, and finally, added, "I'll bring one home, and if you don't want it, I'll take it back."

Frank was not happy, but he stopped arguing. Two days later, I picked up my grandchildren and drove to a shelter for Yorkshire terriers, knowing full well that Frank felt railroaded into getting a dog, but I felt I had little choice. Our delight at watching those tiny puppies scurry to greet us about made my heart burst. We chose one and planned to return in two days to bring her home.

I never did bring her back to the kennel. She weighed barely six pounds, the perfect weight to nestle onto Frank's lap and into our hearts. She was the alarm system that never failed. No one ever got to our breezeway again without my knowing it.

By late September, the days are getting shorter, the nights are cooler, and there is a smattering of red and orange in a few trees, a sure sign that New England's fall is coming. Two cords of split firewood are delivered and stacked, reassurance we will have our fireplace to keep us warm on the coldest of nights and when the power goes out during nor'easters. The flowers alongside the pool have now gone to seed. Lynne and her family are settled in Washington. I return to band practice for the fall semester with longtime friends, and I resume watercolor painting classes. Once again, we have our routine.

On a warm afternoon, while driving to the hospital for blood work, Frank says, "I've been thinking about taking a cross-country trip this spring, maybe a couple of months, get away from blood work, CT scans, and all that. What do you think?"

"On the road for two months? Is that what you mean?"

"Yes."

"Where would we stay?"

"Motels."

"What about Persy?"

"We'll find motels that take pets, and I'll pack my cameras. Maybe make Arizona our destination for a month."

"Hmm…" is all I can think to say. The parking garage for the hospital is ahead of us.

"Well? What do you think?"

Still, I have no answer.

We pull into the parking garage, and I work through options for travel that would make sense for us, knowing that if we do not plan this trip now, there may not be a later time. Not only are possible night sweats, fatigue, loss of appetite, and pain on our horizon, but in a few years, we will be in our eighties and may not have the energy or desire to trek across the country. I sense time running out.

"Well?" he prods again, as though this is an easy decision. But it isn't; I'm not a great car traveler, and Frank knows this. I get carsick and try not to beg to stop and walk, and I seem to be hungry when there's no place to eat. We find a parking space and head for the elevator to the hospital's oncology floor. As we walk the long corridor, hand in hand, Frank lowers his voice, leans toward me, and says quietly, "Remember when you and Jeannie were determined to teach me how to ski down a mountain? And I told you that learning to ski at age forty-eight would be a real challenge for me since I'd never been on skis?"

"I do." This is an odd time to bring up something that happened twenty-five years ago, during the first winter we were married.

"Why are you asking me this now?" We find an empty bench by the window and sit.

"You and Jeannie taught me how to snowplow, how to stop on those slippery steep trails? Do you remember that?"

"Right."

He looks at me with raised eyebrows.

"You took me up the chairlift—first time in my whole life, mind you—and told me I was ready for my first run. Remember?"

I do. The day was cold, the snow well packed and icy in places. Since we had spent most of the day teaching Frank to snowplow, it was late in the day when we finally took a chairlift ride to the top. Sun had melted the snow on the trail earlier, and now afternoon shadows quickly turned the slush to ice. Once off the chairlift, Frank and I followed Jeannie to the beginning of what we thought would be an easy trail, certainly a good choice for a novice skier. None of us realized that right after we began our trek down, a ski patroller roped off that exact trail by the chairlift. I looked back at Frank, who was slowly making his snowplows, and to Jeannie, who had stopped a few yards ahead.

"For god's sake, Jeannie, don't tell Frank this is over his head. This is the wrong trail."

With that, she and I stayed close to Frank, saying, "Great job. Wow! Super turn!" Frank never looked up, just kept concentrating on his snowplows. While we were still in sight of the top, a young, muscular, and red-coated ski patroller fast approached us. In perfect form, he stopped alongside Frank and said with a puff of frosted breath, "Sir, I think this is well over your head. Would you like me to get a toboggan?"

Frank looked completely dumbfounded. "What are you talking about?"

"You look like you may not make it to the bottom, sir. You've a ways to go. I'll radio for a toboggan."

"No, I can do it," Frank said, looking confused and searching Jeannie and me for an answer to a problem he didn't see.

"Well, this particular trail is off-limits. There's a rope across the top by the chairlift." He pointed to the top of the trail and looked at me, and then Jeannie, both of us now bookending Frank, and I knew he thought we were reckless to have brought Frank on this slope.

"It wasn't roped off when we started down," I explained, trying to keep Frank calm. The wind had picked up and blew swirls of snow on the trail below us.

"Well, it is now."

"Frank, what do you want to do?" Jeannie asked with measured calmness.

"I'm fine."

"Suit yourself, "the patroller said with another frosty puff of breath, "but I'll be right behind you all the way in case you need assistance."

It took a while for us to reach the bottom, still accompanied by the ski patroller, but Frank held his own and announced, "That's it for me! I'm done skiing on a mountain with my feet clamped into these things."

We sit on the only available bench in the corridor.

"I think I know why you brought this up. I owe you a trip across the country because you were a good sport about skiing."

"You got it."

He pats my knee.

I glance out the windows on my right that overlook the large green area and see no tables or chairs or people enjoying the day. It's solemn in the corridor, like walking into a church where people are craving uninterrupted silence. There are more patients waiting to be seen than any other time we have been here. Frank's blood is drawn.

Thankfully his results are within the expected range, and we leave the hospital after a short easy visit. Halfway home, Frank looks at me with raised eyebrows.

"Well, if we don't go by car, how would we go?"

"Let's look at RVs."

"An RV? Are you serious? A camper?" He exhales with shoulders dropping to make his point. "A metal box on wheels? What's wrong with going by car?"

"Persy, actually. Separated from us in a strange motel room will make her so upset she'll bark and pant until we return from dinner."

It is heartbreaking for me to think about her little body shivering, waiting in strange rooms, and I can't put her through that night after night.

"I am serious about a camper," I say and sum up the reasons, starting with it being our house on wheels. "There would be plenty of room for your camera equipment."

There is no comment.

"And," I continue, "we could make Lynne's new home in Washington our destination before turning back."

"I'll think about it," he says.

In late October, a month after the last blood test, I fly to Seattle to visit with Lynne and her family. For seven days, I tag along for basketball and swimming practice, and piano, violin, and cello lessons. We have lunches at peaceful harbor restaurants that overlook the colorful boats moored at the docks, and I fall asleep in the evening listening as the girls practice their music. Lynne is happy here with her family, and for me, I see her move as no more than a six-hour airplane trip. By the time I leave, we have plans for my next visit in the winter. I am excited for Frank to see this quaint harbor town. Hopefully it will be our destination after traveling across the country next spring.

When I return home, Frank takes my hand, leads me to the dining room table, points to RV brochures neatly arranged, and says he has found one he thinks will be good for us.

"It's small, has a kitchen, bath, dinette table, and lots of storage for cameras and equipment. We can see it this afternoon." He gives me a big hug and says, "The RV is a good idea. I'm glad you thought of it."

"This is a surprise. What made you change your mind?"

"Persy and storage, that's it." He shrugs his shoulders, as if it all made good sense.

Stacked on the table beside the brochures are his books for the trip: *The Illiad*, *The Odyssey*, *Brothers Karamazov*, and two bins filled with AAA maps and books on camping sites in every state. That afternoon, we walk through a 25' class-C RV, discuss the financing, and buy it. The dealership agrees to store it until we are ready to leave in February, right after Frank's next play and his first blood tests of the new year. That is more than four months away, which gives us plenty of time to plan. We know nothing about RVs, campsites, or camping, but it looks easy, and we are excited. Since Frank feels so well, we make no contingency plans for possible illness nor do we research hospitals along the route. We figure the GPS will give us the directions we need. Friends and family are excited and encouraging when we talk about our plans. I'm not sure they would like to travel this way or if they see this trip as something we better do now because who knows what may be around the corner. Either way, we have support.

Before you examine the body of a patient,
Be patient to learn his story.
For once you learn his story,
You will also come to know
His Body.

—Suzy Kassam, "The Maxims of Medicine"[5]

CHAPTER 4

"Let's Take It Slowly Then"

January and February 2015

New Year's Eve has come and gone. Frank has another CT scan; we will get the results when we meet Dr. A. The worst of winter is upon us: snow is piled high along the streets and the sides of driveways, darkness falls early, and it is cold. Already we have over three feet of snow, and another storm is coming. We cannot keep up with the shoveling and plowing, so we hire someone to do it for us. I ask that we be among the first to be plowed out because if something happens to Frank, we will need to drive to the hospital. Odd, isn't it, I think, that I would even ask this since there is no indication that the cancer is spreading. Maybe I am worrying too much, but I do not change my mind, and the snowplow driver agrees that we can be among the first. It will be good for us to spend the rest of this winter in our new RV in the warmth of the Southern states, away from oncology wards, blood draws, and winter storms.

Again we walk down the long corridor on the hematology/ oncology floor for blood work and the latest CT scan results. As soon as I see the reception desks, that feeling of dread starts to wrap around me. My arms fold across my chest, as though protecting myself from approaching bad news. On a bench by the window, a young man is stretched out on his back with his arms over his eyes, shielding them from the bright sun. His pant cuffs have ridden up on his thin hairless legs, and his socks are baggy on his bony ankles. I sigh and try not to stare. We continue walking to the reception desk and find a place to sit. A middle-aged woman, carrying her winter coat over her arm, sits across from us. Her loose-fitting blouse does little to hide a large gauze pad on her right shoulder.

Frank whispers, "It's better being here waiting for information than dreading a procedure."

We enter the exam room and wait for Dr. A., who finally enters, greeting us with a smile and handshake. He asks Frank how he has been feeling, carefully runs his fingers over Frank's neck, under his arms, and around his belly, then sits by his computer.

"The lymphoma is stable," he reports, "but the CT scan shows a cyst growing on Frank's kidney. I am scheduling an MRI for next Thursday." It takes no more than a second for my throat to catch, my breathing to stop, and tears to tumble out. It surprises me that I have no control over this reaction to what I think is cancer spreading.

The doctor looks at me and asks, "Why the tears?"

"I'm scared." It is an honest answer, but when he asks if I worry a lot, the tone of his voice sounds condescending. I do not hide my scowl and look back at him. Surely Frank must be worried, too, but he does not show it, and though I may be far more prone to worry than Frank, I feel justified at this moment. I am not willing to hide it, and even if I want to, there is no grabbing this worry and stuffing it back inside myself.

"Let's take it slowly then," he says and turns to the computer to explain more about the cyst.

"Thank you." My voice is more clipped than I intend. We get no more news from this visit, and an MRI is scheduled. We leave the exam room and head into the long corridor. I see the young man on the bench, still covering his eyes, his thin legs exposed, and feel pity welling up. It is a helpless feeling.

"If this new thing is cancer, what will we do about the camper?" I ask bravely, barely above a whisper, as though talking to myself. Frank takes my hand and says nothing.

On the way home, Frank says, "We should think about selling the house and moving into a condo."

"We've talked about this before but haven't done anything."

"I know, but I'm feeling a push now. We were healthy back then."

"Yes, you're right. This bit about the cyst hit me hard. If something happens to you, I can't keep up the yard and house without your help."

For the rest of the trip home, all I hear are the tires on the road and the rush of a passing car. Our minds are full of questions seeking answers.

Over the next few days, Frank agrees to give up some of his responsibilities as the artistic director at 4th Wall Stage Company and will no longer act in or direct as many plays. He will work through the finances and the logistics of moving: when to put the house on the market, which real estate agency, bankers, and lawyers to use. He has no interest in packing boxes or deciding what furniture to take or working with the movers. I am fine with that. With this plan taking shape, we both feel relief.

When the MRI results come in, we are relieved to learn the cyst is not cancerous, and nothing needs to be done about it. Our plans to sell the house seem less urgent as our attentions turn to traveling in the RV. Still, we start packing boxes and make lists of what work needs to be done before putting the house on the market.

The most interesting thing about
a postage stamp is the persistence
with which it sticks to the job.

—Napoleon Hill[6]

CHAPTER 5

Struggling Campers

Spring 2015

Mid-March, nearly a year after *Uncle Vanya,* we are leaving the cold of Massachusetts for the warmth of the South. Frank is the driver; Persy and I are the passengers.

As the packed camper inches its way down the driveway, I holler, "Stop! You're going to take the mailbox with us!" We miss it by inches, back up, and try again three times.

Persy fidgets. She acts as though caffeine is roiling through her tiny body, giving her energy far in excess of what is needed. I would rather she acted old and sedate, and rested quietly for hours on my lap.

Persy is not our only problem this first day. It is nerve-racking driving the twisting steep mountainous roads through the Delaware Water Gap and the Poconos. We are often inches from sheer cliffs that could easily tear off our side mirrors, which seem the size of flared elephant ears. We barely speak as tractor trailers rock the RV when they pass. We will stay in motels until we reach a destination warm enough to keep water in the camper from freezing.

In the motel in Bethlehem, Pennsylvania, on our first night, Persy yips, paces, and is so restless we give her one of the vet's Valium pills. After it kicks in, she finally eats and drinks but only out of my hand. At 2:00 a.m., she barks at something outside. I wake up and see Frank reading *The Brothers Karamazov.* He's been up for hours. The room heater starts with a loud rattling burst like a diesel truck starting up, shakes the room, and clanks steadily until it turns off. I need earplugs. We need to outrace yet another snowstorm. We picked the wrong time to start this trip, but it is too late to complain and certainly too late to turn back.

The next two weeks are not much smoother. We stumble along, gradually learning which hose is for drinking water and which is for flushing and where they should be attached, how to coil the electrical line so it stays clean in the storage bin, how to make sure the water gauge is working, and what switches turn what on and what off. We make it to warm weather, having traveled through the Blue Ridge Mountains of Virginia, through coal towns in North and South Carolina, and through Georgia and northern Florida. We got this far on our wits, certainly not our mechanical skills—we have run out of cold water, hot water, and propane, forgotten to tighten the storage bins and overhead fans in the rain, managed flat tires with the help of AAA, and bumped our heads on the bed over the cab so often we stop laughing, and curse.

We drive through blistering heat, rain, and wind and the threat of tornados. We camp alongside squirrels and rabbits that torment Persy, shiver at night when we leave vents open, and flee hordes of mosquitoes and hornets until finally, we learn the camper and learn to read our surroundings better. The mountains, prairies, sand dunes, wild animals, sunsets, and sunrises are our days and evenings as we move through Mississippi, Arkansas, and Oklahoma. The more we shy away from the cities, the more we feel this great country invite us to explore further. We laugh, tell stories, and relax in the evenings as we sit outside under the camper's awning, with Persy quiet on either of our laps. Near the most western part of the Oklahoma Panhandle, we stop for lunch alongside a wide-open flat grazing area for cattle.

"I'd say as a general rule, horses get better fences than cattle. Did you notice that?" Frank says with a laugh. With the warmth of the day and calm around us, he adds, "I think we can say we are living life in the slow lane. And I might add, I am finally getting used to the matchbox-sized bathroom in the RV."

"That's good."

"That's better than you think!"

I add my bit of wisdom, "Did you know the great horned owl preys on skunks? It doesn't care about the spray because they don't have a sense of smell. I saw that on a signpost miles back."

"No, didn't know that."

We pack up our lunch, return to the RV, and head west again.

By May, we have traveled 5,629 miles and are now on a highway in Colorado, headed for our next campsite near Denver. Our plan is to head north to Wyoming, Montana, Idaho, then on to Washington State to see Lynne. Our days are going smoothly, so smoothly that when we have no cell reception, which is often, we are not concerned. When I can, I email Jeannie and Lynne and my brothers, send a picture or two, and tell them where we are. There is something to be said for having everything we need right here in the RV.

Before reaching the Denver campground for the night, we see black clouds rolling over the edge of the earth right at us. The thermometer on the cab mirror says twenty-eight degrees. Snow starts falling, but so far the roads are mostly bare, and traffic is moving. Within minutes, however, the wind picks up, causing little tornados in the road, and traffic slows to a stop. We wait. The snow picks up. Wind blows it sideways. The road is slick as we inch forward. I see the reason for the delay. Two cars are in the ditches on either side. Frank and I do not talk. The wipers smudge the snow instead of clearing it, and the heater is as ineffective as the wipers. We should have double-checked the weather when we had cell reception a few hours ago. Two policemen on the road motion us over. Frank rolls down the window.

"Where you headed?" one asks in an abrupt voice.

As soon as Frank says Wyoming, the policeman warns us that a major snowstorm has hit the main road into Wyoming, and making the trek requires chains, which we do not have. Even if we did, neither Frank nor I could put them on.

"You'll have to turn back," he says quickly with a flick of his wrist.

Frank calmly tells him we have reservations at a campsite a few miles north.

"Okay then," he says and motions us ahead but not before standing next to the rolled-down window and telling us to drive slowly, the weather will only get worse. The drive to the campground is slow with near-whiteout conditions. We never expected snow in May. I can feel my heart pumping and know Frank's is also. For once, Persy is asleep on my lap.

It is a relief to pull into our campsite, which is just a slot between two other campers, no more than two arms' lengths to our sides. The temperature has fallen so fast that we need our down coats, mittens, and boots, which we have not used since leaving Virginia thousands of miles ago. We leave Persy inside as we hook up the hoses for drinking and wastewater, and attach the cord for electricity. Frank's fingers are white, so I take off my mittens to tighten the hoses as he blows warm breath into his hands. When all the storage bins are secured, we head inside, turn on the heat, and try to think through the next steps. I check my cell phone for a weather forecast, but there is no reception.

"We'll wait out the storm and see what happens," Frank says. "We have plenty of food and water, and if the electricity doesn't go out, we'll be fine."

"I'll take Persy out now before the snow is too deep for her, then make dinner," I say.

"Stay near the camper," Frank shouts out the door.

After dinner, I go to bed to read. I am glad this day is over and hope we don't get snowed in for days. Persy is snuggled next to me.

By morning, the sun is bright, and the storm is over, but we can't see out the snow-covered windows. I put on my coat, grab a broom to clear the windows, and head outside. The snow is deep and trickles into the tops of my boots as I walk around the RV. Other travelers are doing the same clearing and assessing, while the man next to us is on top of his camper with a hairdryer, trying to repair the hole a tree limb made when it crashed down in the night. Maybe he is trying to melt some kind of repair fabric.

That was close, I think, *too close.*

Then as Frank is drinking his morning coffee, he says, "I fell asleep last night at the dinette table after working on photo prints." This is not unusual. "When I woke up, my heart was pounding furiously, and I had trouble breathing. It lasted for fifteen minutes. I thought I was dying."

"Dying? Are you serious? Why didn't you wake me up?"

I am frightened, but what would I have done if it had been an emergency? With no cell reception, there's no 911. The central office for the campground is about a mile away. How would I get there in this snowstorm? We had never discussed what we would do in an emergency like this. We simply never questioned that one of us might not be healthy. I am sick with worry for Frank.

"I don't know," Frank says. "Didn't seem necessary."

"Do you want to go to a hospital now?"

"No, I feel fine. Slept well."

"Do you think it might be the cancer?"

"No, I don't have those symptoms."

We look at each other, take some deep thoughtful breaths, and I say, "I think we should forget Wyoming and leave for home as soon as we know the roads are safe."

"No, I think we should backtrack and find another route north."

"Look, you just said you thought you might be dying. I am not waiting for that to happen while we are on the road in this camper, thousands of miles from home. You need to see a doctor."

He lets out an exasperated sigh, but I don't care; I hold my ground. He agrees reluctantly, and as we finish breakfast, we talk about resuming our trip next spring, certainly later in the year than when we left this time.

When the campground is cleared, we finish packing, take Persy for her last walk of the morning, start the engine, and leave. Though the trek home for Frank is not what he hoped for, he's relaxed and glad to take a northerly route. For me, I check off each state we pass through—Colorado, Kansas, Missouri, Illinois, Indiana, Ohio, Pennsylvania, New York—anxious to reach Massachusetts. It is tedious and takes nearly a week to arrive home.

As promised, Frank sees his primary care physician, who tells him that if the difficulty breathing and racing heart happen again, he should call 911 immediately. Fortunately Frank's electrocardiogram is normal, as are the other tests, even the forty-eight-hour heart monitor. There is no mention of cancer, and our lives settle into the routine of spring.

We look at condos but have not found a suitable one. I pack boxes of things for the eventual move and stack them in the basement. Contractors paint and fix up the interior of the house. I sign up for the next semester of band. Frank is feeling fine, and neither of us is concerned. September's oncology visit is uneventful: Frank's blood work levels remain within the expected range. He has no pain, fatigue, night sweats, or appetite loss, so he remains without treatment. Meanwhile, maps, books, and notepads are on the dining room table again, ready for our next trip in March, less than six months away. Maybe this time we will make it to Wyoming and then on to Washington.

The trouble is you think you have time.

—Buddha[7]

CHAPTER 6

Land of Floods

Winter into Spring 2016

January's blood work is fine, but this winter is awful. For three months, heavy snowstorms hit Massachusetts, one after another, making it one of the worst winters in history. Finally in late March, right after we learn Frank's blood counts are fine, we hitch the Jeep to the camper and leave a good twelve hours before the next snowstorm is predicted to hit the northeast. An accident on the highway costs us precious time to outrun the storm. By the time we reach a motel in Pennsylvania for the night, the snow has started falling. If the storm is heavy, we may need to spend the day here and wait for the roads to clear. By morning, with only a few inches of snow on the parking lot, we are so relieved that we have a leisurely breakfast, answer emails, and relax.

We casually travel through small southern towns, try barbecued ribs, marvel at slow-swimming manatees, squish our toes in sugary white sand on Florida beaches, and take our time meandering through outdoor art shows and indoor museums. We walk marked trails in swamps, open grasslands, and mountains. Our life on the road is free of doctor visits and blood draws, heavy coats, and boots. The past health episode in Denver, when Frank thought he might die, is not a concern now; and though we realize some unimagined issue might arise, we have no contingency plan other than to address it when it happens. It has taken us a long time to adjust to camping, but we are finally taking our time to see what we want, to marvel at the unexpected, and relax in the evenings as we recount the past days and plan the next.

At one small town in Georgia, we park the camper and walk the only street with stores, most of which are boarded up. As Frank walks the street with his camera slung over his shoulder, Persy and I sit on a bench by the only stoplight at the edge of town, and watch the cars go by. The day is warm and bright, and I try not to feel awkward sitting here as though I have nothing to do. I do feel awkward, though, because it is true. I have nothing to do but enjoy myself, sit for as long as I want, and have an ice cream cone if I want. Passersby wave, smile, whistle, or point a finger. We are the oddballs in town, standing out among everything familiar.

Frank joins us with two cappuccinos, puts his arm around me, and says, "Well, I guess we are finally campers."

Who would have thought this little town would have cappuccino? I stick a bit of foam on the tip of my finger and offered it to Persy. Right then, a tall thin man walks by. He stops, leans to pat Persy, and says, "Aren't they just a joy, these little Yorkies! Make you want to get off the couch and go outside. Just a joy."

I open my mouth to brag, but he was off.

We are in Selma, Alabama. On a warm bright afternoon, Frank sets up his camera and tripod on the Edmund Pettus Bridge while Persy and I walk to the Old Depot Museum close by to learn more about the sad riveting history of this small town. Frank meets us for lunch at a restaurant with outdoor seating overlooking the Alabama River. It's peaceful sitting here with Persy on my lap, enjoying the fresh air, and eating a lunch I don't have to prepare.

"Was the museum interesting?" Frank asks.

"It was. Want to go there after lunch?"

Frank doesn't answer. His face is pinched. "What's wrong?" I ask.

"Just a pain in my side." He straightens in the chair, looks at me, jerks when he takes a breath, and then lets it out and smiles. "It's gone now."

Lunch is leisurely. Afterward we go to the museum. In a back room filled with exhibits of the violent history of Selma, I know something is not right with Frank. He's quiet and winces a couple of times. I ask again if he's all right.

"Yeah, just that pain in my side."

"Do you want to go back to the camper?"

"No, it comes and goes."

That evening, Frank complains again of pain, takes a Tylenol, and sits at the dinette with Persy snuggled next to him.

"Probably pulled a muscle when I lifted the groceries yesterday," he says. Neither of us thinks the pain might be caused by cancer. Who in their midseventies doesn't have a pain or two every now and then? Only six weeks, ago his blood counts were fine, and no one at the hospital expressed any concern. In a few days, we plan to walk the streets of New Orleans and listen to jazz. Before bed, I take Persy for her walk. Frank chooses to stay in the camper.

By morning, after more Tylenol and Motrin, the pain is still there.

"Where is it?" I ask. His fingers go directly to his left side and move cautiously around the area just below his ribs.

"It's not that bad when I take the pills, but I think it's a good idea to take it easy today."

I am worried that if Frank is unable to drive, I will have to, and I do not want that, especially on the heavily congested Northeast Corridor.

"Maybe I pulled a muscle," he says again.

We leave Alabama and, for the next two days, travel through most of Mississippi, avoiding southern routes along the Gulf Coast, which has been pelted by heavy rains and severe flooding. These are long rainy days spent almost entirely in the camper, but we make good time, hoping to cross the Mississippi River and arrive in Louisiana sometime tomorrow. We sleep well.

By morning, the rain has cleared, and within an hour of travel, we are at the Vicksburg Bridge, a four-mile connection between Mississippi and Louisiana. What a sight! Below huge cargo ships move steadily upriver and down. We agree to find a parking spot by the river for a walk and lunch. Frank's pain seems more manageable with Tylenol and Motrin. He hasn't minded the hours of driving to get here and seems happy to leave the camper and walk to the river.

The narrow wooden walkway that juts over the river seems safe enough, but I don't like it. The water is black and bottomless to me. We are the only ones here except for hordes of mosquitos and overhead vines that seem otherworldly. I am sure they conceal snakes that might drop onto my head. A large cargo boat slowly moves on the huge river with the silence of a submarine. Could there be alligators here, their bodies motionless in the water, their eyes on us? The air is still.

"This place gives me the creeps. I swear there are snakes in those vines?"

Persy tugs on her leash to get closer to the water. I pick her up and hold her close to my chest. Frank doesn't answer me. I turn and see him holding his side, slightly bent.

"We need to get home," he says, "The pain is worse, and I can't seem to control it with Tylenol or Motrin."

A silent shudder passes through us. I hold my breath. My god, this pain is happening fast, and for Frank to show concern and the need to get home quickly is enough to set me on a near-razor-sharp edge.

"I think something is wrong," he says. "I can't drive the RV home. We'll have to take the Jeep." For a few minutes, neither of us talks. "I thought the pills would take care of it, but now I don't think it's a pulled muscle, and the pills are helping but not completely."

We look at each other, our minds trying to process so much at once: the pain, the sudden intensity, what to do with the camper, and how quickly we can get home.

"We need enclosed storage for the camper. Someplace that won't flood," Frank says.

I watch him open the camper door and slowly climb the stairs. He sits at the dinette, puts his elbows on the table, and seems to catch his breath. I take out my computer, hoping to find the names of enclosed storage facilities, but there is no cell reception.

Frank is breathing slowly; his eyes are closed.

"You stay here," I say. "I'll take the Jeep to find cell reception and make a list."

"No, I'm coming with you."

"Do you want something to eat before we go?"

"No, I want to get this figured out."

It takes time to find reception in this part of flat swampy Louisiana. We make numerous calls but find no enclosed storage. By now it is 6:00 p.m. No one answers our calls. We return to the camper.

Meanwhile, our time is consumed with packing clothes for the trip home, cleaning out the refrigerator and freezer, and leaving everything else behind for when we return to continue our trip. As the pain worsens, Frank's movement is slower. He winces even when sitting. I can finish up all the packing myself and tell Frank to get comfortable wherever he can—the dinette, the bed, the cab. Our space is confined with few options. I fix dinner for the last time, I hope, and take Persy for her walk. We cannot afford to wait much longer.

Early the next morning, we finally locate an enclosed storage garage in Louisiana in a flood-free zone. By lunchtime, we have driven for hours in rural Louisiana in search of stores with battery chargers, locks for the storage door, and mice repellant. That evening, we back the camper into the enclosed storage, attach the battery chargers, spread the mice repellent, and lock the door to the storage bay. I write the lock's combination in my diary. We fill the Jeep with gas and leave for home.

For three days, we trade off driving; Frank takes the morning shift when the medicine is its strongest, and I take the afternoon shift. Each afternoon, we find a restaurant for dinner, and a motel. After three days of steady driving and two nights in motels, we are home. It is April, six weeks after we left Massachusetts, and nearly two years after I sat in that theater's back row watching Frank walk across the stage, and saw a lump on his neck large enough to cast a shadow. I am relieved to be home, to be near our doctors, and to have family nearby. It is only now that I realize how fragile we were traveling so far from home and from everything familiar and safe.

Serious illness is never experienced in isolation. Our social nature as humans turns our individual battles into family ones, and like battles, the wounds are borne by all on the battlefield. The formal diagnosis for these wounds is "caregiver stress." It is an inadequate term that encompasses myriad manifestations: anxiety, weight loss, gain, fatigue, insomnia, etc. To support the patient with serious illness, their care team must also be healthy, and it is vital to address the issues that come with caregiver stress.

—Dr. Nancy T. Skehan, MD[8]

CHAPTER 7

Nearly Fatal Assumptions

April 2016

Within a week after arriving home, Frank's primary care doctor orders an endoscopy, colonoscopy, and blood tests. They all show nothing of concern, so he orders a CT scan next. The intermittent pain is so bad now that sleeping and sitting are difficult, while other times, it almost goes away. The pain medicine is not always effective, but his primary care doctor is reluctant to prescribe stronger medicine. Frank pleads but is denied.

Meanwhile, the house is cleaned, polished, and on the market. When Frank is not in pain, we look at condominiums, but we cannot find one that checks all the boxes: a south-facing end unit with sun and light on three sides, and bedroom and laundry on the first floor. We are kicking ourselves for waiting so long.

Frank returns from an appointment with his primary care physician with news that the CT scan results show follicular lymphoma growing rapidly in more than one area in Frank's abdomen. He will need treatment if he is to survive. This is that desperate moment we hoped would never come. We traveled through the Southern states nonchalantly, thinking more about our tomorrows on the road than our yesterdays of blood draws. The primary care doctor finally prescribes a stronger painkiller that helps, but we question why he waited so long to order the CT scan. The effects of the painkillers take time to work and do not last long enough to cover the pain until the next dose. The side effects of excruciating constipation are alarming, so the primary care doctor orders additional medication to help. The cycle of pills, pain, constipation, and foggy thinking is frightening, though Frank suffers in silence. I don't think his lack of complaint is for my benefit; I think that is how he faces this illness, inwardly and quietly. Perhaps his Vietnam War experiences have carried him through to now.

We see the oncologist next week. While I am in the basement packing boxes for our move, Frank is often upstairs sitting on his chair in the living room, with Persy on his lap. He is less interested in theater, photography, almost everything. Jeannie visits when she can, and when she cannot, she calls. Just hearing her voice is a stabilizer, and knowing she is there to help, if only for a few hours, tamps down some of my fear. It is the same when Lynne calls, and though she is on the other side of the country, I know that she would be here on the next plane if I asked. They both are worried about Frank.

Finally we have an offer on the house and have found a condo we like but have not heard back from the owners to know if our offer is accepted. We should have pushed harder a year earlier to plan out this move. Too many issues are tumbling around us right now, usurping what reserve we have. We are tired. I am frightened.

When friends call, and I tell them the latest news, I feel their silence wrap around me as surely as if they were standing next to me with arms outstretched, but we do not have words to penetrate the quiet. They ask how Frank is doing, and I say, "The medicine is helping with the pain. That's good. We see the oncologist next week."

When they ask about me, I say, "I'm fine."

I do not tell them my stomach is in knots, that being on alert is exhausting, sleeping is a problem, and that I don't know where we will live once the house is sold. What could they do to help me other than worry more? Then a day before our appointment with the oncologist, the seller accepts our offer on the condo. If all goes well, we should close on the sale of the house and the purchase of the condo at the end of June.

My concern now is that Frank is well enough to sign papers at the closing. If not, I have the power of attorney. As we review the documents we will be signing in a few weeks, Frank looks at me. His face is calm as he tells me, "I don't want you to have to deal with the bank and attorneys on your own. I'll do everything I can to keep my energy up and make sure we go together. I need you there, and you need me to make sure everything is in order. We're going to do this together."

Again we walk down that long corridor of the oncology wing to see Dr. A., and as before, I wonder if tables and chairs might appear on that island of green outside. The few pictures on the wall are the same ones I had seen before, those splats of color, but now I would not stop to look at any picture, even if it might draw me in. I do not care what is hung there; I only care what the doctor will tell us. We sit by the large windows, as we have so often, but the air today feels different from all the other times. We both feel it. I close my eyes and breathe slowly in and exhale, asking God or a spirit or otherworldly being to stay close, to protect us, to make this easy. The uncertainty of that happening all but negates the prayer, and I exhale.

Frank's name is called; we are ushered into the exam room and wait until finally, Dr. A. knocks quietly on the door, as though he does not want to disturb us; just a gentle nudge to tell us he is about to enter. He smiles, shakes our hands, and then motions us to sit. He, too, is surprised the lymph nodes have grown so rapidly, especially the large node that is pushing on Frank's intestine, those nodes around his pancreas, and those in the mesentery, which is the supportive tissue of the bowel. The cancer is not in the pancreas or bowel. He tells us again that follicular lymphoma is not curable. We know that, and we know it can transform into another type of cancer, but neither of us think to ask if it has, and Dr. A. does not mention any transformation.

We also learn there is a large cyst on Frank's spleen, and Dr. A. orders a PET scan. This particular scan has a special dye containing radioactive tracers that will collect in areas of high-chemical activity. Since cancer cells have a higher metabolic rate than noncancerous cells, they will show up as bright spots on the scan. Dr. A. prescribes continuous-release morphine for the pain. Frank also needs chemotherapy to stop the growth of this cancer. Chemotherapy will not cure it, only knock it into remission if we are lucky, and that is the best we can hope for at this point. I am worried about Frank surviving chemotherapy. If the chemotherapy doesn't put the cancer into remission, he might not make it.

As I sit in this small office listening to Dr. A. explain the treatment, something does not feel right. I look at Dr. A., in his white coat and badge, sitting at the computer trying to explain to us what the computer image tells him, but neither Frank nor I can make sense of it. I think Frank may be complimenting him when he says it must have taken quite some time to learn how to read a screen like that. Dr. A. smiles. My gut is telling me that we should not stay with this doctor or hospital. Why, I ask myself, after we hurried home from Louisiana, did it take these doctors so long to find this rapidly growing cancer? We wasted those weeks of tests prior to the CT scan. Knowing Frank's history, why didn't his team suspect cancer immediately? And what is as upsetting as these thoughts is the fact Frank received a strong painkiller only after the CT scan. So many weeks of pain. I don't understand how this happened.

My insides are churning with anger, so much so that I'm having trouble focusing on what Dr. A. is saying. He is talking to Frank, almost with his back to me. My face feels hot. I stand, take a step toward Frank so I can see Dr. A. as clearly as he can see me. He remains seated, discusses the chemicals, and points to the computer screen, but I am not listening any longer. Something inside me feels frozen in place, as though it just stopped, as though I'm in free fall unable to control any of what has happened or will happen. If I did not think to ask if the pain might be cancer weeks ago, what other questions am I not thinking to ask now?

Just then, Dr. A. swivels his chair to face me and says this would be a good time to see the infusion floor, where Frank will have the chemotherapy administered.

"Let's have a look," he says.

I interrupt, "We are closing on our house and condo the last week in June. I'm not sure how Frank will feel then if he starts chemotherapy before."

"A good point," Dr. A. answers. "There is no problem starting chemo the first of July. We can schedule that."

We climb the stairs to the next floor and enter another long corridor, but this one is different from the one downstairs. Instead of chairs and waiting rooms, this corridor has many private areas, simply curtained off on both sides and opened to the corridor. They are each the size of a large closet, with a reclining chair, television, window, table, and IV supports that can be wheeled if necessary. It looks bleak. We are told the first treatment will take six to eight hours and will last the longest of all treatments. The doctors will monitor responses to the initial chemo because it can stop his heart. *Oh god, please don't tell me that.* Frank will receive large doses of antinausea medicine.

There will be six cycles. Each cycle consists of three weeks. In all, Frank's treatment will last eighteen weeks. The first week in July, right after we move into the condo, will be the start of the first cycle. On Monday, he'll arrive at the hospital for chemo, the only day of the week for treatment. The next two weeks, he is free. The level of chemo is moderate, Dr. A. says, but it has to be more than minimal to stop the cancer from growing. The pain will stop, he assures us, and Frank should go on with his life, which he calls the new normal. He will get his strength back. I hope Dr. A. is right, but how would I know? Time is the one thing we have now, but we may not have it later if something goes wrong. When the tour is over, we shake hands and leave for home.

I rush to clean out what is left in the house, sell what we can, and hope Frank is well enough to sign legal papers at the bank and attorneys' offices. I make reservations at a local inn one night before we can move into the condo. Frank pushes to help when he can, but his energy reserves have bottomed out. He moves slowly, hunched over more than before, and carries only the lightest boxes. When he isn't helping, he sits on his chair with Persy on his lap. Jeannie helps when she can, but most of the work I can do myself.

The last Saturday in June, the movers clean out everything from our house. The walls echo. This is so hard. I know I am not leaving family behind, just a house, but it has been my haven for twenty-five years. What suddenly hits me is a conversation Frank and I had many years ago, when we were getting to know each other. We had hiked up a narrow rocky mountain trail to the top of a ledge overlooking the White Mountains in New Hampshire. Miles of green forest below were visible on a stunningly bright day.

"Aren't we lucky," he said, "to be able to hike these mountains."

Yes, I thought, but I felt even luckier to have found someone who liked hiking as much as I did.

"My dream for years," I said as I ate the last of my sandwich, "has been to hike all the New Hampshire mountains of two thousand feet."

He looked at me, cocked his head as though confused, and said, "Never thought of that. Maybe. May take a few years. That is, if you're planning on sticking around that long."

"What do you mean?"

"With all your moves from Alaska, New Hampshire, Massachusetts, don't you see yourself as somewhat of a vagabond?"

"Vagabond?" I said, taken aback. "You think I am a vagabond?" I tried to smile and looked at his face, wondering if he was criticizing me for moving from place to place, job to better-paying job, with my sole goal of making enough money to put Jeannie and Lynne through four years of college on my own.

"I do."

As we sat in the gorgeous sunshine looking across miles of green forest and finishing our sandwiches, I was not going to defend myself and could think of no relevant comment, so I made none. Those were hard times and not worth explaining as we sat alone on the side of the mountain. We were both in our early forties then, both divorced, and just beginning to learn about each other, both very reluctant to wade into past relationship failures. On the way down the mountain, Frank stopped, took off his backpack, and invited me to sit next to him on a fallen thick branch, resting atop two boulders, a seat in the wilderness, a place of privacy.

"I'm sorry," he whispered, putting his arm around my shoulder, "if I spoke out of turn."

I looked at him and decided to say nothing. Instead, I leaned into his shoulder and gently nodded my head. It felt good to feel his body close to mine and to know that he had sensed my pulling away.

Now standing in an emptied house, with nothing to sit on, no cup for tea, no cornet resting by the piano, I know how fortunate I have been to have had the security of this home for these twenty-five years. I shrug my shoulders at the vagabond label and call Persy, knowing that for this move, I am not alone.

As soon as the moving van leaves the driveway, Frank and I leave and lock the door behind us for the last time. Frank will drive to the inn, and I will drive to the kennel where Persy will spend the next two days until we are moved into the condo. We will sign all the legal documents tomorrow. When I get to our room at the inn, I realize the reclining chair we requested is not there, the one for Frank to use in the night when the pain is so bad that he cannot sleep. I make sure that before we leave for dinner, a chair has been brought to the room. Begrudgingly two men from the hotel staff lead me from floor to floor looking for the right chair, and when we find it, I walk behind the heavy lifters as they bring it to our tiny room. As I slip under the covers this evening, I know tomorrow will be stressful, but it will be a relief to sign the papers and move into the condo.

> No matter what you do, you will very likely come to a point where you feel that you have failed your loved one in some way…At those times, it is important not to blame yourself.
>
> —American Cancer Society literature[9]

CHAPTER 8

Chubby Hubby

July to October 2016

Week 1: The first day of chemo. I've packed food that Frank would snack on under normal conditions: a sandwich, applesauce, peanut butter crackers.

Frank's infusion room is simply walled off by curtains and no less dreary today than the last time we were here. I feel sick to my stomach knowing what he will be going through, but there seems no reason for me to stay for eight hours. As the nurse inserts the IV and attaches a tube to his arm, she tells me he will be very tired and may sleep most of the day. Frank looks quite relaxed, leaning back in his chair with his feet up, looking stronger than he has in days. He takes my hand and says, "I think you should go back to the condo, take care of Persy, and try to relax. I'll call when I'm ready to come home."

Before I leave, I ask when the doctor will come to make sure Frank doesn't die with whatever drug they give him. The nurse assures me that that is taken care of and that I am welcome to stay if I wish. Frank says he is fine, that I can leave. I gently squeeze his free arm, tell him I love him, and with a pounding heart, I pull back the curtain, pass the nurses' station, and press the button for the elevator.

When Persy and I walk the paved sidewalk at the condo, there are friendly hellos, but that is the extent of the conversations, and I am fine with that. I don't know anyone here, and right now, I am much happier by myself. We have asked friends not to come by because we don't know how Frank will do with the chemotherapy. We need time alone to adjust to these changes.

I like the condo, but with no gardens for escape, it's confining, and I don't know what else to do with myself once I am home. Upstairs I have a studio with a desk for watercolor painting and a desk for writing. Boxes are everywhere, but I've not much interest in organizing any room other than the bedroom, bathroom, and kitchen. My piano is in the dining room, too heavy to move elsewhere, and my cornet rests on its stand.

Jeannie calls to see how I am, and again I say, "Doing okay, but don't worry about me." She asks that I call when Frank gets home.

At the end of the day, Frank calls and says he feels okay. I leave immediately for the hospital and promise myself to not pepper him with questions in case he is tired. I park outside the hospital entrance and watch Frank walk to the car. He looks fine, his gait is normal, he is carrying a large paper bag, and he smiles when he sees me.

"How are you feeling?" I ask when he is in the car.

"I'm not tired, and I don't feel nauseous, but I want to get home to use our bathroom and see Persy."

"What is in the bag?"

"Notebooks and pamphlets from the Cancer Society."

The door closes, and we head home after day 1 of week 1. I call Jeannie. We have the remaining six days of this week and two more weeks after that before the next chemotherapy.

"What do you say we go to New York City in two weeks?" Frank asks.

"You feel well enough to do that?" This is a surprise.

"Not yet, but the doctor said I should in about ten days. That will give me time to get some of my strength back. Plus, the painkillers are working, and the constipation is better. I think it would be a good idea to see some museums and get out of here. We haven't been there for a while."

"Are you sure?"

"I'd like to stay in Midtown Manhattan, where we always stay. It's near the museums, and getting taxis won't be a problem."

"Why don't we wait a couple weeks, then decide. It seems a risky trip if you start to feel awful from the chemotherapy."

"No, Dr. A. assured me I'll be feeling better. So let's plan it."

"Okay," I agree.

So by the end of the second week, we travel to New York City and stay in Midtown Manhattan. Most of the morning, we walk and rest, go to a museum, stop for coffee, and are grateful to be able to do this. Early afternoon, though, we return to the hotel for a nap. We talk about resuming our camping trip across the states in the fall, after chemotherapy ends. We remember a camper we met in Mississippi who traveled for two months, then returned home for cancer treatment, then left to travel again. Couldn't we do that? Maybe we will sail through cancer and chemotherapy.

After chemotherapy 2, Frank is doing well. He still plays golf and goes to rehearsals three times a week for the play *My Name Is Asher Lev*, which opens in September. He has energy, is eating well, and looks good.

By September and chemotherapy 4, things are slowly changing. Frank does not feel as well. He is eating less, sleeping more, and pushing to make it to some rehearsals for the play. When he returns to the condo after one rehearsal, he heaves a heavy sigh, and says, "I snapped at an intern. I'm sorry I did, but after three rehearsals showing up late, not completing what is expected of her, I told her if I can be going through chemotherapy and feeling sick, certainly she can try harder to carry her weight."

"What did she say?"

"I don't know. Really don't care right now. I'm too tired to do her share of the work as well as mine. Who knows, maybe it will do her some good to know she is not measuring up."

"Well, it isn't like you to snap," I say.

"I know." We leave it at that.

Sometimes he picks at his food, even the comfort foods, and sometimes he will eat everything. When a full meal is overwhelming, I suggest cereal or macaroni and cheese, fried eggs and toast, or oatmeal and containers of rice pudding, anything to keep his weight up. His ribs, hip bones, and cheeks are starting to poke out. When I mentioned this to Dr. A. at our last appointment, he chuckled and, with a glint in his eyes, said "Get some Chubby Hubby."

"What is that?" I don't think this is funny.

"Ice cream. He'll love it. He needs to eat whatever he can keep down."

Is this really true?

We try Chubby Hubby, but he doesn't like it. Later that evening, after watching Frank struggling to eat, I say, "Frank, I think we should get an appointment at Dana-Farber. At least get a second opinion."

"No," he says in a weakened voice. "We have one of the top oncologists here. It's close by. I'm not changing doctors. Please don't ask me to do that."

"I understand, but Dana-Farber is one of the world's best cancer hospitals, and it is close enough for us to drive to."

He looks at me, pleading not to press further.

Still, he's up every morning, meeting rehearsal schedules a couple times a week though reluctantly, and working on photography. His energy and spirit are slowly draining out of him. Vomiting is now an issue, and Dr. A. orders medicine to counter it. Frank says his thinking is sometimes fuzzy, and blames all the medicine.

I am concerned my own thinking may be fuzzy, too, but I do not confess to anyone. If I need help for a few hours, it is there, but not for days; and that is enough for me to always say, "I am fine." But on those sleepless nights, when raw dread blankets me as I check to see that Frank is still breathing, I am not fine. I make a plan to call 911 if there are any changes, to switch that responsibility from me to EMTs. On the nightstand beside my bed, I secure the phone with a piece of sticky gel so that it cannot be knocked onto the floor and land behind the nightstand, out of reach. With that much of a plan, I am able to sleep.

By morning, when the sun finally streaks through the windows, I look in the mirror and think I am fine, just tired, which I tell myself is okay for this kind of stress. After a cup of tea and some breakfast, I feel sure that I am okay. At least Jeannie and Lynne, my closest supporters, do not suspect otherwise, and that is enough for me.

As we get closer to the next chemo infusion in August, Frank is weaker. He is throwing up more, his appetite is diminished, and he is losing more body mass. His hip bones, back bones, and shoulder bones are even more prominent.

"Is that weight loss expected?" Jeannie and Lynne ask.

"Yes."

"How long will this go on?"

"It will probably get worse as the chemo continues. The doctor is ordering all sorts of medicines to counter these reactions. They should be helping."

"Doesn't sound like they are."

"It's not only that. He still has pain in his side. It comes and goes, but it's still there regardless." I am close to tears, trying to hide them in my voice, but I cannot. "I don't know what else to do." Then I hear those reassuring words of comfort.

"Mom, you'll be okay You're strong. You are doing all you can do right now. You let us know what we can do. But meanwhile, get some rest, take care of yourself."

"I know, but…"

"But what?"

I take a deep breath and tell her that a close friend called and suggested I go to a medical library and study everything about this cancer so I'll be knowledgeable when we are with the doctor.

"Well, that's just great! What does she expect? That you'll earn an emergency medical degree? If I were you, I would tell whoever that was to back off!"

"You're right." I exhale.

On a sunny day in the last week of August, when Frank is sitting on his chair in the living room, with his eyes closed and breathing slowly, I sit beside him and take his hand. "Do you remember when we first met at the Chamber of Commerce breakfast meeting, twenty-eight years ago?" Persy snuggles deeper into Frank's lap. "We were seated at the same breakfast table with six others. There must have been a hundred people in that room. You probably knew them all. I didn't know a soul."

Frank nods.

"It was my first day working with the Chamber of Commerce. I was so frightened I would be asked to speak that I couldn't eat, and knew I would throw up if I did, and then I heard your deep voice across from me, saying something about your awful cooking, that you lived alone and had no one else to blame. Everyone laughed, but I just kept looking at you."

I feel him squeeze my hand.

"You were so handsome with your black hair and immaculately trimmed mustache, dressed in a dark-gray suit, and those silver cuff links on your white button-down shirt."

He turns his head to look at me.

"Without checking, I knew your shoes were polished to a shine." I pause. "And tall. You were taller than anyone else." I wait a bit. "I did have to speak but had nothing prepared and tried to avoid your eyes as I stood at the podium, floundering. I think that is the moment I fell in love with you."

Frank's squeezes my hand again and says, "You did okay."

"We're going to get through this," I whisper. "I know you don't feel well, but we'll get through this."

He nods and releases my hand.

At my watercolor class later that week, Jeannie calls my cell phone to check in. I immediately walk out of the art room into a cold, dark, unfinished stone corridor. I blurt out in tears that I am very worried about being alone for the rest of my life. She listens, says she loves me, she's always there for me, and tells me to go back to my class and paint. I do, relieved not to have to talk anymore about this, but the sadness does not ease up, and I pack up my paints and paper and leave early.

Tech week, the week before the play opens, is grueling, with rehearsals every night. If Frank had listened to me, he would have asked someone else take over his role, but he did not listen, and tonight he is onstage for the opening performance. From where I am seated, in the back row, I cannot tell that Frank is tired or that he has undergone chemotherapy for the past thirteen weeks, but I am certain that if he loses his concentration, he will fall asleep. There is a standing ovation after the last lines. I'm glad this performance is over and that we can go home.

Dr. A. attends one performance, which is not surprising because at every appointment, he and Frank discuss literature and theater and exchange books. Dr. A.'s presence brightens Frank's spirits as he is now a friend and supporter, an equal lover of the arts. Camaraderie is not something I feel for Dr. A. Our common interest is Frank, and I am not sure his medical expertise is enough.

The first week in October is chemotherapy number 5. Fall is coming. Some leaves are turning red. The midafternoon sun is still hot, but that will change soon. We close the windows earlier in the evening now. The benefits of condo living are clear: it is far easier to press a button for heat than to haul in wood for a fireplace, the lawn is mowed and raked by someone else, and it is reassuring to know that we can live on the first floor if Frank is too weak to use the stairs.

The pain in Frank's side is getting worse, and heavy doses of morphine and oxycodone are now routine. The constipation is again painful and alarming. Nausea, vomiting, and gut-wrenching fatigue are constant. Didn't we expect all this, especially toward the end of chemotherapy? We discuss this with the doctor and nurses on the infusion ward, and they tell us this is normal. It will take time for Frank's body to rebuild bulk and strength. He should be feeling better soon. But how soon? They say it will take time. We need to be patient. His body has gone through a lot. This is how it is.

It's one thing for me to be told this and quite another for me to see how Frank's body is reacting. How much further does his body have to struggle before it begins to strengthen?

We see Dr. A. on the oncology floor shortly after the last week in October, when the final round of chemo is complete. He tells us that Frank's blood work is fine and that every level is in the expected range, but he is concerned about the recurring pain in the area of the cancer. It should not be there at this point, so instead of waiting for a month to pass, which is the protocol, Dr. A. orders a CT scan for next week. There is no mention that the cancer may have transformed to another type of cancer, and I don't ask about it. I feel a surge of overwhelming helplessness.

Only once before can I remember feeling this helplessness, and then it was my own fault as I had chosen to climb a mountain in New Hampshire late in the day. By the time I reached the treeless summit, all other hikers were on their way down. The light was fading, and I was alone, unable to distinguish which cairn was the one for my trail. I screamed for help, but no one was there to hear me. I forced myself to remain calm and focused on the cairns at the various trails, trying to remember something, anything, about the one I had passed a short while ago; but the shadows were strengthening, and I was scared. Eventually I recognized something familiar on one cairn and headed down the mountain in near dark to the safety of my car. That feeling of helplessness was a good teacher; I never lost my way again on a mountain.

If I could focus on something to lead me through this helplessness now, as I had focused on those cairns, my fears might calm, and I might find my way through this uncertainty; but right now, I don't know what that is. I just have to wait and hope Dr. A. is making the right decisions.

Caregivers can have many negative feelings about their role. They can feel angry, guilty, sad, and anxious. It's important for caregivers to know that this *is okay.* It is essential for caregivers to have the space and the community to process these feelings, which ultimately are reflections of grief for what's lost when lives are upended by serious illness.

—Dr. Nancy T. Skehan, MD[10]

CHAPTER 9

Forty-Pound Drop

For the next week, as we wait for the CT scan results, I rarely leave the condo except to shop for food and medicine. I retreat into painting, playing the piano, and doing scales on my cornet. Ginni, a friend down the road in another condo, stops by to check in. Often we simply sit with tea and knit. Talking right now seems an effort.

Jeannie also stops by when she can. Her hugs bring me to tears.

Frank has now lost 40 pounds. His bones are sharp against his skin, and his ribs are easily countable. He looks sick. He weighs 147 pounds, down from 187 pounds before treatment. His thick black hair has fallen out, his voice is weak, his face is puffy, and his appetite is almost gone. I watch him sit hunched over a plate of food, elbows on the table, hands supporting his head. He picks here and there; and eventually, when he puts something in his mouth, I know it is not enough to sustain him. He says he'll try later and returns to his chair in the living room, where he sits or sleeps with Persy on his lap for hours. Persy does not leave his lap, day after day, and when I try to take her for her walk, she rearranges her little body to snuggle deeper into Frank's lap. She knows Frank is very sick. He shuffles, bent over as he walks, his neck and shoulders drooped like a very old man. I am watching him slowly die. I don't know how to help.

Jeannie knows my anguish and tells me to make an appointment with Dana-Farber Cancer Institute in Boston. When Frank wakes from his nap, I tell him again that it's a world-class hospital for cancer research and care, but he says no, that we have the best at this teaching hospital, it is close to home, and he refuses to make the drive into Boston in case of an emergency. I am loath to push him at this point.

In the midst of this, we get a call from the hospital telling us that Dr. A. has left his practice. We receive a date for our first meeting with the new oncologist, two days away. Just like that. Nothing from Dr. A. Nothing. We are stunned. Frank retreats to his chair, his fatigue and nausea outweighing his disgust and disappointment. I write down the number for Dana-Farber.

"Frank, please listen to me," I say softly. "I'm calling Dana-Farber now to make an appointment. I don't think we can wait."

"No," he snaps. "Not yet."

"No, I think we should call Dana-Farber."

"Please, I can't argue." His eyes close. "If Dana-Farber does not accept me, we need this new oncologist as an ally until we are certain about Dana-Farber."

He drifts from me.

There is something about Frank that will not be pushed. I have learned this after some rough spots in our marriage. Right now, I think I am right about calling Dana-Farber, but if Frank feels forced, it will only compound his stress and make him dig his heels in further. Reluctantly I agree to wait until we meet with the new oncologist.

Once again, we walk down that long corridor, more anxious than we have ever been. When we meet the new oncologist, Dr. B., she says hello to Frank but looks past me, as though I have no relevance, no voice, or perhaps a voice she doesn't want to hear. I think she may be overwhelmed by taking on some of Dr. A.'s patients without time enough to study their cases. She speaks quickly, seems to listen intently, and moves on to new subjects when she's satisfied with what Frank is telling her. There's barely a breath between her questions and Frank's answers, and I am on edge trying to absorb all that is being said. I know she doesn't see me as part of Frank's team. She asks the same questions Dr. A. asked: How are you feeling? Where is the pain? Her voice is clipped, rushed.

Given the sporadic pain in Frank's abdomen that should be gone after eighteen weeks of chemotherapy, she is concerned the cancer may be wrapped around the splenetic artery or that the cancerous lymph nodes are not as reduced as we had hoped. She wonders aloud if radiation may be the next step in controlling the cancer and pain. She never mentions the possibility that the cancer may have transformed, and I am too upset to remember all the symptoms. She tells us the CT scan will provide some answers. I ask if she will call us as soon as she has the results and certainly before we are to meet again next week. She says she is not sure. I am so sick of waiting for results. This is not right. Just like that, the visit is over.

During the next two days, nothing changes. I speak with my primary care doctor about my anxiety. I have little appetite for food, I am losing weight, and sleeping through the night is difficult. She tells me these are normal responses to the stress I am experiencing, and tells me I must take care of myself. I am trying hard to figure out what that means when Frank sits nearly all day in his chair and tells me he is not sure he will make it. I am tired, strung tight with worry, and see no relief. Everything has been downhill so far. When I have to buy groceries or prescriptions, I hurry so that Frank is not left alone for too long. I watch him sleep, making sure his chest rises and falls. His face is so bloated I barely recognize him; his whole body has changed. I am desperate to know this treatment is right.

"Frank, we should call Dana-Farber to see if we can get you in."

"No, not yet. I've already told you we need this doctor as an ally if Dana-Farber won't accept me. Wait until we get the CT scan results, please. Please!"

"But we don't know Dana-Farber won't accept you. I'm going to call."

His voice is soft but abrupt, "No, damn it!"

"Well, I don't trust these doctors anymore," I say and walk out of the room because I am too close to saying something I might regret. *You've gone through weeks of chemotherapy, you still have pain, you look sick, pale, weak. You look awful. Dr. A. let you down. He let us down. Your bucking me is making me really mad. I know I am right. I am not going to let you die! You are being a jerk!*

The day after this imaginary conversation, Frank nearly falls when he walks into the kitchen. He grabs the counter, leans over to catch his breath, then shuffles to a chair where he sits, eyes closed, breathing short quick breaths.

"What's going on?" I ask, gently holding his shoulder.

"The vomiting and diarrhea are awful. There's nothing left inside me," he says in a whisper.

This is more than I can handle. In one day, he has gone from being able to wait for the next doctor's appointment to totally exhausted and probably severely dehydrated, and if I don't get him to the emergency room soon, I am afraid he will die. While he sits in the kitchen, I rush to the bedroom to pack a small bag of his clothes, slippers, toothbrush, and toothpaste. I fill Persy's food and water bowls.

"Frank," I say, "get up out of the chair, grab my arm, and hold tight. I am taking you to the emergency room." I expect him to say no, so my resolve is steady. If I have to call 911 to force him to the emergency room at the hospital, I will. Instead, he nods his head in complete compliance.

We walk slowly to my car. I open the door for him. He shuffles his body onto the seat. I hand him the small bag of clothes he may need if admitted, and some food for us if we have to sit for hours in the waiting room. His eyes are closed the whole trip. Once we arrive at the admitting desk, I show the red card that indicates he is a cancer patient, and he is wheeled into an exam room immediately. The helplessness of being a bystander is overpowering: Why did I wait so long to get help when I knew in my gut that something was wrong weeks ago? Why did I even care what Frank thought? Is it my fault he may be dying? My knees nearly buckle under this weight.

Frank is admitted. The stress of this day has sapped my energy and goodwill. It is a relief to hear him suggest I return home rather than sit in the chair by his bed for the night. When I arrive home from the emergency room, Persy runs to me with such excitement that for a few moments, I forget everything but the wonder of this little dog jumping onto my lap and tunneling her nose into my neck. She all but pulls the stress from me. I take a sleeping pill my doctor has prescribed and sleep all night with Persy snuggled against me, thankful Frank is in the hospital and that I am free from checking to see if he is alive.

Early the next morning, I take Persy for a quick walk, and return to the hospital. My heart is pounding as I ride the elevator to Frank's floor and wonder how he survived the night. I knock gently on his door and find Frank sitting up in bed, looking rested and more alert than yesterday. I see the back of a man, dressed in a white coat and a stethoscope around his neck, standing beside the hospital bed. He and Frank are talking. I stand aside, not wanting to interrupt, but Frank does that for me. As he introduces me, he says, "He took one look at me last night and said this is not right. He is a radiologist. Dr. B. asked him to see me." The radiologist explains he believes the chemotherapy Frank has been given has not treated his particular cancer. I'm trying to take all this in, to make sense of it. It's astonishing, I think, that he could tell this at a glance.

"At a glance?" I hear myself say over and over. "At a glance?"

The radiologist tells me he is ordering a biopsy to confirm his suspicions and that Frank will have to remain in the hospital for the biopsy. While he discusses possible radiation treatments, it is all I can do to hold back my anger. I feel my lips pressed into a slit as the enormity of this discovery hits me squarely in my stomach. We made a life-threatening decision to trust Frank's medical team. I am stunned that no one ordered a new biopsy when Frank was obviously in more pain, getting thinner, weaker, and almost too disheartened to care. How does this happen?

As soon as I get home, I am calling Dana-Farber. If Frank thinks our waiting was a mistake, he does not say so, and anyway, it makes no difference to me now what he thinks. What matters is that we get to Dana-Farber. I leave for home.

"My husband has been diagnosed with follicular lymphoma and has had four and a half months of chemo, but he has recurring pain, and we are concerned the cancer has not been treated correctly. He is weak and very thin. Could I please make an appointment with someone to see him?" I say when I place the call. I answer the requisite questions, and I have an appointment in three days. They will request all Frank's medical records; there is nothing we need to do except arrive for the appointment.

I stand up, raise my hands, and shout, "By god, we are going to Dana-Farber." The tears fall on their own, and I do not stop them. I call Jeannie and Lynne and my brothers.

When we first meet people, understandably, they are very shocked. They've just received a diagnosis that may significantly alter their life. And although we review all the information with them about the diagnosis, treatment, and what to expect, not surprisingly most people don't process all of that…And so it is helpful to have a caregiver…there who's hearing the same information…who can help the patient know what to expect going forward, and for that caregiver to anticipate what to expect going forward so they can help, coach, and guide the patient through the process, in addition to us coaching and guiding the patient through the process.

—Dr. Eric D. Jacobsen, MD,
division of hematologic malignancies,
Department of Medical Oncology,
Dana-Farber Cancer Institute

You may encounter many defeats, but you must not be defeated. In fact, it may be necessary to encounter the defeats so you can know who you are, what you can rise from, how you can still come out of it.

—Maya Angelou[11]

CHAPTER 10

How Much Time Is Left?

On December 15, 2016, I help Frank into the car, and we leave for Dana-Farber in Boston. If it is not rush hour, the trip is short of an hour; if it is rush hour, it is over two hours. Most of the drive is highway. Fortunately the roads are cleared of snow, traffic is light, and we should arrive in under an hour. Frank sleeps most of the way in, and I am grateful my GPS tells me where to go. I am somewhat familiar with Boston, but not the Longwood medical area, home to Harvard Medical School, Dana-Farber Cancer Center, Brigham and Women's Hospital, and Beth Israel Deaconess Medical Center. The hospital parking garage is well marked. I drive down four floors to the first available parking space, help Frank out of the car, find the elevator, and we finally reach the lymphoma floor. Frank checks in, has a bracelet attached to his wrist, and is instructed to sit in the waiting area. With nearly a half-hour wait for our appointment, we instead walk to the lobby where there is live piano music. We sit among a small gathering of listeners. The music is soft and gentle and flows inside me. I get lost in these measures of calm, grateful to have these moments. Eventually Frank nudges my elbow, and we leave for the lymphoma floor.

This waiting room is larger and brighter than the one in the other hospital, more open with one wall of windows. All the patients here are adults. Some wear gloves and surgical masks covering their mouths and noses. Some are in wheelchairs. All the patients are accompanied by a helper, someone either listening for a name to be called or rubbing a sore shoulder or leaning close, whispering. I breathe relief in this waiting room. Though I know no one, I sense a connection and feel that Frank and I make a team just as those around me do. I think my fears are similar to theirs; my nights and days are like theirs. If I started a conversation, we would connect and share and reassure. I belong here.

When Frank's name is called, we are ushered to an exam room and wait in silence. Dr. J. arrives with a smile and friendly handshake. He is much younger than we are and is dressed casually in a button-down shirt and slacks and comfortable shoes. He's calm and has a slight chuckle that makes me relax and listen. When he sits and finishes looking at the computer, he faces Frank and asks how he's feeling.

"Okay, considering," Frank answers in a weak voice.

Then we wait. There is a silence while the doctor seems to calculate the chances for Frank's survival. After reviewing Frank's medical records and the latest biopsy results, he tells us the follicular lymphoma has transformed to diffuse large B-cell cancer, which requires a different treatment. No one casts blame or criticizes decisions made by the other oncologists. That seems a waste of time right now, though I can feel my body tighten and my heart race. He explains the three options for Frank's survival: more chemotherapy, radiation, or a stem cell transplant.

Dr. J. waits a moment.

"My recommendation is for stem cell transplant," he says with a slight nod of his head, "but we need to be sure your body can withstand the treatment." He speaks gently, waits for the information to filter, and is ready to explain further, but Frank interrupts.

"What are the side effects from the other treatments?" Frank exhales the words, and we both stop breathing until the doctor answers.

"With the other treatments, there's a possibility of cognitive damage—"

Before he finishes this sentence, Frank's voice is stronger than it has been for weeks, and he says, "That is not acceptable. I will not have any treatment that impairs my thinking. I would rather die than have that."

The doctor says he understands, but we have to find out if this new cancer, diffuse large B-cell, responds to a new chemotherapy. If it does, Frank will be a candidate for stem cell transplant.

"I don't understand what has happened," I say. "Does he still have non-Hodgkin follicular lymphoma?"

Dr. J. explains that he still has the follicular lymphoma, but part of that follicular lymphoma transformed into diffuse large B-cell, forming a tumor. There is a good chance this new cancer can be cured, but the non-Hodgkin follicular lymphoma is considered a chronic, incurable disease. His voice is calm, not unlike Dr. A.'s, but I sense something different, perhaps that he would not joke about Chubby Hubby or criticize my tears, and that he would be aware when a different treatment is needed.

Dr. J. explains that it has only been recently that patients in their seventies have been allowed into the stem cell-transplant program, and those who are included must be otherwise healthy. In January, which is two weeks away, Frank will be admitted to the hospital for three days of chemotherapy. He will have his own room during this process, and visitors are allowed. Dr. J. explains he will receive a chemotherapy regimen called R-ICE. The purpose of this chemotherapy is to see if the diffuse large B-cell cancer responds prior to the stem cell transplant. If that happens, it tells us that the cancer is more likely to respond well to the high-dose chemotherapy associated with the stem cell transplant.

I wait a moment to let this sink in, then ask, "And if it hasn't?"

Frank places his hand on mine and whispers, "Let's hope it has."

"If the cancer does not respond to R-ICE or another similar regimen," Dr. J. continues, "then the transplant is not likely to work."

"What are the other options?" Frank asks as he exhales.

Dr. J. explains that with additional chemotherapy, Frank would have 25–30 percent chance of getting rid of the diffuse large B-cell cancer. Organ damage is also possible.

"And with the stem cell transplant?" I ask.

"Frank will have a 60 percent chance of resuming a normal life."

A moment passes. Dr. J. thoughtfully says, "Some patients don't make it through the transplant." There is a long silence as Frank and I look at Dr. J., who nods his head slightly and waits, and then says it is an outcome we have to be aware of.

"He might die," I say slowly under my breath, less as a question than as a fact. This moment is resignation. We have come this far, through chemotherapy and near death, and here we are at Dana-Farber, with another option that seems to give as much despair as hope. Again under my breath, I say, "He might die."

"The most common life-threatening side effects of transplant are infection or severe organ damage from high-dose chemotherapy," Dr. J. adds, "but he is strong for his age." I watch him nod his head and look at Frank. He moves his lips in a way that, at any other time, may have been the start of a smile, but it is not a smile. I am reading his expression as one that says, *There's hope. We are in this together. We will do all we can.* He waits to make sure we understand this. I think we do. I guess we do. I'm not sure about anything anymore.

We leave the office with information on stem cell transplants, take the elevator down to our car, and drive from the bowels of the parking garage to street level. I start to memorize the route home. In a few days, we will be returning to admit Frank for three days of chemotherapy. I anticipate driving in and out each day to visit Frank. Traffic is stop and go. We are anxious to see Persy and be in a safe place that provides comfort, though we are tense and the condo and Persy can do little to erase these feelings of dread. We need a buffer between life as it was and life as it is, if only for a short time. When we arrive home, Frank retreats to his chair in the living room; I call family and friends. Once again, I hear the same silence, intake of air, slight moans, and overwhelming wishes of hope and good luck.

Early Christmas morning, we return to the hospital for a shot that is a prerequisite for the upcoming three days of chemo. The shot is called Neulasta and is designed to accelerate recovery of white blood cells that fight bacteria after chemotherapy. It will give Frank a chance of reducing the risk of infection. What a treat to walk into the hospital waiting room this morning and find no one else here. It seems odd to have the choice of any seat, to sit alone. Maybe because it's Christmas morning.

A nurse comes into the waiting room and ushers Frank away. It takes only a few minutes for Frank to get the shot and return. Had we not been here, we would be home, passing the hours until leaving for dinner at Jeannie's. Lucky us, I think, the timing is right.

On our way home, the air is cold, snow is packed against the sides of the roads, and the car heater is whirring. Frank sleeps with a blanket over his legs and chest. I turn the temperature up. He looks fragile, almost too tender to touch.

Once on the highway, my memories take over. He was strong in his twenties: a dissertation away from a doctorate at Emory University, an army first lieutenant in Vietnam, and later, when I knew him, president of an insurance agency and the Chamber of Commerce, and my golfing partner. The event that strikes me as vividly as though it were happening at this moment is an annual Chamber of Commerce dinner in 1988. I was the executive director of economic development for a group of towns in Massachusetts, and Frank, as president of the Chamber of Commerce, was the moderator for the evening agenda.

As usual, the speeches were too long with too little substance. Finally after the last speaker, we were ready for the evening to end, but it didn't. Frank stood confidently at the podium and waited for complete silence. Not a fork clanked on a plate. All eyes were on him now as the pause was longer than it should be, making us wonder what was next. He then leaned into the microphone and announced to the entire audience that he wanted me to come to the podium. I pushed back my chair, walked forward in my best suit and heels, and wondered how red my face must be and if sweat was seeping onto my jacket. I had no idea what this was about. Frank looked at me and smiled, then announced that I was his fiancée. There was an audible hush (the local newspaper reported an audible gasp) in the audience, then wild applause. He handed me a dozen red roses and kissed me. Time stopped. My heart raced. I held the roses across my arms and walked back to my table. I put the roses on my lap, and for the rest of that dinner, my mind drifted to the comfort of our intimate peace and place, something neither of us had experienced for years.

We arrive home to Persy's frantic greeting. Frank naps while I take her for a walk before we leave for Christmas dinner. At Jeannie's, all of us gather in her kitchen, while Frank retreats to the sofa in the living room, where a fire is throwing a warm glow across the darkened room. I'm sure Jeannie has closed the drapes because she knows Frank might want to rest there. No one says anything, but we all know this is serious. One by one, we leave the kitchen to check on Frank. When dinner is served, Frank is not hungry, and we leave early.

Once home, seated in his chair with Persy on his lap, he says, "I sensed people were saying goodbye to me. They knew, and I knew, I might not see them again."

"I think you are right." I then ask, "Are you afraid of dying?"

"No, I'm not. I feel a peace when I think of it." He nods his head, as though agreeing with himself. "I fear the pain but not dying."

I leave for the kitchen to make scrambled eggs and toast, put the plate on a tray, and return to the living room.

Frank pulls a blanket over his chest. "I was thinking about Dr. A.," he says. "I don't think I was real to him. He easily could have dictated a letter or sent an email saying he was leaving his practice. It would have acknowledged a relationship."

"Yes, you're right."

"I see him much like I see an actor who has memorized his lines but doesn't know how to get involved in the play, doesn't understand the emotion of the words, or the power of relationships. That kind of actor makes the audience an outsider, unable to participate, and that's the shame of it."

Later that evening, Frank stands at the kitchen counter, sobbing. He hands me an opened envelope Jeannie gave him this afternoon.

> *Frank, I took a moment this holiday season to think especially hard about what you might like for Christmas. I thought about warm socks or gloves and decided those types of gifts were not going to work. This year something completely different is in order. I know you are going to get through this and have many more years ahead to enjoy life as part of our family. I also know that you have been and will continue to be a big part of my life and my kids. We respect your thoughtfulness, your perspectives, your writing skills, and just being part of "us." This is a coin my grandfather gave me. I know if he were here he would put his hands on your shoulder and pray with you and for you. He was the luckiest and most optimistic person I have ever known. This is a small piece of his legacy. I want you to keep it close to you to remind you how much we all are rooting for your recovery. We all love you very much. Love, Jeannie.*
>
> *Oh, I forgot, you may have to sterilize the coin.*

PART 2

SWAYING

It's common for family members and caregivers
to experience increased stress throughout
the transplant process. In addition to worry
and concern about you, they may also be
dealing with work, children and household,
finances, as well as burnout and exhaustion.
It's important to recognize that your caregiver
may need to take a break from time to time,
so that he or she can best provide for you.

—Dana-Farber health information materials[12]

CHAPTER 11

Cured, Ruined, or Dead

January 2017

On New Year's Day, I need to find a place for peace and clear thinking. I can't think of where that would be, so I try deep breathing, counting my breaths in and out, practicing my music longer, knitting, and painting. None of them helps me feel any peace. Maybe I need something outside of myself to absorb this dread. Perhaps I should contact the hospital volunteer department to see how I might help. I wonder if patients might like to dictate something that I could write on my watercolor notecards to be sent off in the day's mail. Perhaps they will get a handwritten note in return. Or maybe I'd knit caps for those who have lost hair. My thoughts of volunteering skip through my consciousness like flat rocks skipping over quiet water. So I return to my deep breathing.

A week later, before the snow starts, we return to Dana-Farber for blood work and a meeting with Dr. J's assistant. As we begin the trek from the lower level of the parking garage up to the eighth floor, the elevator is not crowded, but by the time we reach the lymphoma floor, the elevator is packed. I check the directory for each floor: cutaneous oncology, radiation oncology, head and neck oncology, hematologic malignancies, leukemia, melanoma—the list goes on. So many floors. So many cancers. No one talks. We inch our way to the front to exit.

The eighth floor waiting room is crowded. Nearly all the seats are taken. Some people are in their twenties, some middle-aged, some elderly. Some are in wheelchairs, some are very thin and bald, wearing masks and gloves. Others appear to have no outward signs of illness other than their bracelets, just like Frank when he was first diagnosed. We find two chairs together in the back, and sit and wait. Frank tries to read, and I try to knit. Minutes nudge tediously forward on the clock. Frank nods off. To my right, a man, who is obviously a patient, is hunched over, eyebrows knitted, as though in pain. Beside him, a woman is reading a Kindle in one hand and, with her other, rubbing the man's shoulder, as though she has done this a thousand times before and knows just where it hurts.

Within a couple hours, Frank's blood test results are available. There is no waiting for days to learn the results. With the news that Frank's levels are within expected ranges, we leave the hospital for home, no closer to knowing yet if Frank will be admitted into the stem cell program. We don't discuss any what ifs. Frank rests quietly against the car seat, a blanket over his lap. He seems too weak to keep his eyes open. I listen to classical music on the Boston station.

Once home, I have to get out of the house to breathe in the cold air, clear my head, and listen to the quiet stillness around me. I step over icy patches on the sidewalk, stuff my gloved hands in my pockets, and breathe through my scarf wrapped around my neck and chin. The first snowflakes of this next nor'easter are falling lightly. It will be bitter in a few hours. This peaceful quiet just as the storm begins is what I need, and I could stand right in this spot for a long time. Persy cannot, however, and tugs to return home.

Later, when the snow is blowing sideways, and wind is whistling around the kitchen windows, I take out the stem cell-transplant notebook. For the first time, I read aloud what Frank may be facing, step by step.

When I finish reading most chapters on the process and side effects and discuss them with Frank, he says, "How about that! Looks like I'll be cured, ruined, or dead." It is a light moment.

The next day is cold, with brilliant sun reflecting on a foot of fresh snow. Tree limbs bend, birds flit from feeder to feeder, and plows grind along a road in the distance. We greet others walking their dogs.

"If you are able to have the stem cell transplant, you'll be in isolation for three weeks. What will you do?" I ask with dread.

"I've already decided," Frank says through the scarf across his face. "If I'm accepted, I'm packing books and downloading movies."

"What movies?"

"*Indiana Jones* movies. They are mindless adventure. I like them." He stops walking, takes my hand to stop me, and says, "And I will wait for you to visit."

We just stand there, leaning against each other on the sidewalk, until Persy pulls on the leash.

"All I want is to be with you, hope my hearing and kidneys are not affected, keep working at photography and theater, and stay as close to normal as possible when it's over."

The days pass. Frank is eating more, asking for meals he likes, and gaining weight. If this keeps up, he will be even stronger if he is admitted for those three weeks in isolation. This is so encouraging that I feel my guard letting down and my muscles relaxing. I even catch myself breathing air deeper into my lungs and taking my time to exhale.

My watercolor classes are mostly quiet. The painter who sits next to me shares information about her husband, who has just been admitted to the hospital. A look in her eyes is enough for me to know what's going on. We lean on each other without words, just smiles and silent wishes for better times. Sometime into January, I write to tell her our good news, that Frank may be admitted into the stem cell-transplant program at Dana-Farber. I hope she is well and painting. She doesn't write back. I learn her husband has died.

On January 13, Frank is hospitalized at Dana-Farber for three days of chemotherapy to see if the diffuse large B-cell lymphoma responds. His room has a bed, chair, bathroom, large blackboard, TV, and IV stands with bags hanging from hooks. He says he feels strong and talks about food, but within an hour of my visit, he starts to nod off. I feel pressed to leave before rush hour traffic so I can take Persy for her walk and check in with family. The rest of the day and night is a relief from worry and vigil. I sleep well with Persy snuggled by my feet.

The second day of chemotherapy, I would prefer to stay home to catch up on laundry, food shopping, mail, and bills, or just sit and read, paint, or play my cornet. I want to withdraw from everything and everyone. Maybe I am just tired. But when I think of Frank alone in that hospital room, with drugs dripping into his vein, I pack my lunch and leave.

He is much the same as the day before: in bed with tubes reaching to needles in his arm. He is in such a fragile state, attached to tubes, completely dependent on others for care. His eyes are closed, and I feel I should not stay long. He is tired, and while my presence is a comfort, I can tell he will drift off to sleep shortly. I leave for lunch in the cafeteria, and by the time I return to the ward, he is asleep. With a gentle nudge I tell him I am leaving for home and will be back tomorrow. He nods his head. I leave quietly, close the door, gather up my coat at the nurses' station, and leave all of this behind for the rest of today. By the time I accelerate onto the highway and head home, a wash of relief takes over. Traffic is heavy, so I drive the speed limit in the right lane. The car is warm, the gas tank is full, and I feel a sense of peace I have not felt in a long time. Frank is in the best of care, and the rest of this day and night are mine. I'll change the bed, put out fresh bath towels, and make chicken with mashed potatoes and peas for tomorrow night's dinner when Frank comes home. He will like that.

The next day, Frank is relieved to open the condo door and see Persy jumping to see him. At dinner, he stops eating, takes my hand, and thanks me for the dinner.

"It's good," he says and finishes every bit of the chicken and mashed potatoes and peas.

Two days later, we return to Dana-Farber for more blood work. I remind Frank to tell the assistant about the pain in his side that has not gone away. As usual, nearly all the chairs are full. Some patients would fool you they look so good, but the white wristband gives them away. The heartbreakers are the very elderly couples, one with a knitted hat or scarf to cover a scalp now bald from chemotherapy, another looking just too old and worn down to go on, and some so old and weakened that pushing their sick spouse in the wheelchair seems to consume about all their energy. Maybe the younger ones look at Frank and me that way. Today's blood results are all in the expected range, and blood tests are now twice a week.

At home that same afternoon, as I try to watch a YouTube video on stem cell transplant, the doorbell rings. It is Jeannie and my granddaughter Alex.

"This is perfect timing," I say. "I couldn't watch much more of that video. I'll finish it later."

Alex is sixteen, with that tall long-legged body many runners have. She hands me a present, a betta fish in a bowl filled with water. Its colors are blue and purple. She puts it on the kitchen counter and says, "This is for you." Her face is sad. "It might help to have something small to take your mind off everything."

We hug, and then Jeannie puts her arms around us. I ask them to stay for a moment, but Alex has a track meet. The three of us are wiping tears. It is such a hard time for us all.

"Come with us, Nana. The race starts soon. I would love to have you there."

"Yes?" I look at Frank. He insists I go. This is a healthy break.

At the meet, Jeannie and I stand on the balcony overlooking the indoor racetrack. The high school distance runners are lined up, the gun goes off, and I follow Alex as she moves around the track, passing the other runners. She is light on her toes, and her long blond hair bounces off her back. Her face is red with determination, and I join the applause when she crosses the finish line. Afterward I send her a poem starting with Limerick, the name we gave the fish, asking how the race went:

Limerick asked how you did at the race.
Asked if Hermes helped pick up your pace.
As the Greek God of Speed,
He could nudge when in need,
But, I said you aced your own pace in the chase.

Alex tells me she has pinned the limerick to her bulletin board, and I am happy about that. The next time we see Dr. J., we learn that he, too, is concerned about the recurring pain in Frank's side. The PET scan cannot be scheduled any sooner than next week because a specific amount of time has to pass to allow the cancer to react to the chemotherapy. If we learn the cancer reacted to the chemotherapy by next week, Frank will undergo stem cell transplant. If it has not responded, we do not know what treatment to consider.

As I wait for this important decision, time drags. I meet Betty, a fellow trumpet player from band, for lunch, and afterward we play our trumpet duets and a few New Orleans' jazz pieces, the easiest renditions we can find. We stumble and start over but keep at it until we play nearly every measure together. I love these times.

Frank is tired and withdrawn, spending much of the day at his computer or napping. He said he is steeling himself for what he might be facing. He has lost all his hair, his posture is bent, and he is out of breath walking up a flight of stairs. When foot and leg cramps are severe enough to awaken him, Frank will retreat to his chair in the living room to finish out the night, and by morning, I'll find him rubbing his head.

"It's amazing how much insulation that little bit of hair had." He laughs. "I need watch caps, the kind fishermen or the navy sailors on guard duty wear."

"I'll order wool caps."

"No, they have to be cotton. Wool's too itchy."

I miss Lynne. She repeats often that if something happens to Frank, I can live with her and that I will never be alone. If I don't want to fly, she will come get me and fly back with me. She will always have a place for me.

We don't know what to do about the camper parked in Louisiana and decide to keep paying storage fees, knowing that eventually, we will return and head further west, maybe early next summer. Right now, however, we have a strong tether to Boston and no intention of going any further than the forty-five miles between Dana-Farber and the condo.

Finally the day for the PET scan is here. We arrive early morning at the hospital. While Frank has the scan, I wait in the lobby for an hour until he returns. We have lunch in the hospital cafeteria. There is not much to say now. Later in the afternoon, we are called into Dr. J.'s office. The seconds barely seem to budge. I hear Frank sigh. We both fidget in our chairs until finally Dr. J. opens the door and greets us.

He asks how Frank has been, then turns to the computer and pulls the scan results up on the screen. He tells us the tumor is not visible, but the scan is not powerful enough to see all the cells. It is much like pricking a pin into an orange to hit a seed, he says; not all pricks will hit a seed. Still, he recommends the stem cell transplant. He reminds us this will give Frank a 60 percent chance of resuming a somewhat-normal life, and that if Frank were to have only additional chemotherapy, he would have a 25–30 percent chance of getting rid of the cancer and would face the possibility of major organ damage. Age is an issue, Dr. J. adds.

We will start the process the end of this month, beginning with prerequisite exams: pulmonary function, a dental exam, electrocardiogram, lab work, urinalysis, and a chest x-ray. If Frank's results are not where they should be, he will not qualify for the stem cell transplant.

"And who will be the caregiver?" the doctor asks, looking at me.

"I will. But what does that mean?"

"Frank should be able to bathe and dress himself when he gets home, but he'll be very tired. He'll need his meals prepared. He won't be able to go shopping for about two months and will not be allowed near people for six weeks. The main issues are fatigue, infection, and illness. Someone needs to be with him to make sure he is doing okay, that he gets his medicines, the house is clean, and to let us know if that's not the case. He'll need to be driven to the hospital for follow-up blood work and tests."

"Yes," I say. "I can do that."

"Fine," Dr. J. says. "I expected that. But there's one more thing. I need to know that you have a caregiver."

He looks at me expectantly.

"A caregiver for me?" I straighten in my chair. "What do you mean?"

"In case you're unable to care for him, is there someone you might be able to call on? Someone whose name you can give us?"

I stumble. There is no one I can think of who could take over if something happens to me. Jeannie works full time, as does Lynne, and I have no friends who would be that free; all are busy, and most work. A huge weight rests on my stomach, and I feel near panic. I should have made more friends, joined some clubs and a church, been more outgoing. That's not my nature, but I should have done it anyway. I stumble with my thoughts in disarray. My heart is beating faster, and I am sure my face is either flushed or pale.

"I'll need to think about that," is all I can manage to say. "No one comes to mind right now."

The doctor nods his head and moves to another subject. Frank takes my hand, as if to say, *Please don't worry. We'll be okay.* Oh god, I better stay healthy and on top of things.

A day later, Ginni, my condo knitting friend, stops by for tea. We sit in the kitchen, both of us quiet, both of us knitting. It's that way with Ginni; we can sit for hours, knitting or reading, and not speak. It's a new type of friendship for me.

"I have a problem," I say.

She looks up, eyebrows raised, and waits for me to explain.

"I need a caregiver for me—"

Before I finish the sentence, she raises her hand. "Of course I'll be here for you."

That's it. I tear up. She stands to hug me.

As the days pass, Frank eats more, gains weight, and takes longer walks. He feels well enough to drive us to the grocery store and wait in the Jeep while I go in. At home, he can sit for hours processing photographs, a dramatic change from just a couple of weeks ago. He suggests I make reservations to see Lynne in Seattle and assures me he is well enough now to take care of himself while I am gone. Our next appointment at Dana-Farber will be the battery of requisite exams. It will be a long day, and because the tests begin at sunrise, we will spend the night before in Boston. With this in mind, I make plane reservations as far out as I can, planning to arrive back home in Massachusetts the day before the tests begin.

Life seems to go on without effort
when I am filled with music.

—George Eliot[13]

CHAPTER 12

Violins and Nor'easter

On the six-hour flight to Seattle, my seat is by the window and next to a very heavyset man whose foot creeps into my space. Already his thigh is an inch on my seat, but I don't want to touch it. I nudge his foot with my toe; he does not budge. His eyes are closed, and his mouth is open. I nudge his elbow on the armrest to get his attention. I'm sure he is pretending to be asleep, so I nudge him harder.

"Could you please move your foot?"

He does, but moments later it is back. I tap his arm with a bit more urging and nudge his foot with my toe. Finally when he moves his foot again, I block it with my backpack. Now with my coat tucked between my shoulder and the window, I close my eyes and try to think of nothing. I want to relax, but what comes to mind are those people who say to me, "Oh, he'll be fine. Don't you worry. They're making great headway to beat cancer. And you know what? My sister beat her cancer, so I know Frank will beat his. You'll see. Cheer up."

I want to say back, "Please, your comparisons are not helpful." And when I hear, "Read. Read. Read all you can about cancer and treatments," I don't know how to respond to this overwhelming homework assignment either, so I don't. I'll escape these conversations while I am visiting Lynne. Unless she has told her friends about

Frank, no one will know, and that will be a relief, if only for a few days.

I try to imagine what the force of cancer might look like, maybe an invisible stranger walking beside me, gripping my upper arm with tight fingers, like a police officer might grip the arm of a captive. I want to pull away, but I cannot; its fingers push too hard into my muscle. It forces me to walk at its pace, not mine. Yes, I think, that's how I see it. But there is something else about cancer that I see every time we are in the hospital waiting rooms, and it has nothing to do with seeing ourselves as impotent captives. It is that exceptional urge to survive, to find treatment, and hope the decisions trusted doctors make are the right ones. Then you pray and hope with all your heart that you have chosen the correct path, one that may be painful and unpredictable, but one that eventually runs its course, and you'll be fine. You want to beat the odds, come out on top when it's over. Isn't that why we endure the blood draws, doctor visits, tests, chemotherapy, and radiation, as well as the pain, nausea, and constipation? Yes, that thought seems to me the right one for me at this moment. I hold onto it as I fall asleep, my head against the window, my feet free to roam the little space I have, unimpeded by the foot of the man beside me.

As I walk outside from the airport terminal, Lynne waves from her car. Her smile is everything to me.

"You look good, Mom," she says. "The girls can't wait to see you." I nod. I am happy. "We don't have extra stuff planned, just the usual school stuff, afternoon sports, and music lessons. We just want you to hang out with us," she says.

The days are too short, and my energy lags, but I hang on through the music lessons, swim meets, and basketball. My most favorite times are rehearsals for Youth Symphony and evenings at home with violin, cello, and piano practices. My upstairs bedroom is a haven after these busy days. I just need to put my feet up, I tell myself, but the truth is, I have no more energy. As I sit on the bed with my back against the pillows, I hear the pleasing sounds of Bach's "English Suite" on the piano, then Ravel's "Concerto No. 2 in D Major" on the cello, and then Mendelssohn's "Hebrides Overture" on the violin. How lucky I am to sit, close my eyes, and listen. Then like clockwork, after their practice is complete, I hear the patter of feet on the stairs, and I know these three young musicians are coming to say good night to me, but it's more than that. They climb onto the bed, rearrange the pillows, and for the next hour, we chat and laugh and catch up on middle school and high school in their new town. I love being here.

Lynne pokes her head in and says, "They can't get enough of you."

On Saturday, the day before I'm to head home, we are in a Tacoma church where rehearsals are held for the Youth Orchestra. Lynne and I sit with other mothers in the church hallway at the welcoming table. Just around the corner from us is the large room where the young musicians rehearse. The church vibrates with cellos, violins, and violas. Then I overhear one mother say, "Wow! New England is getting clobbered again with a nor'easter. Probably a couple feet this time. Bet they're setting records this year!"

"When?" I blurt.

"Oh," she says casually, "starting tomorrow, Sunday, late morning and lasting all day. It's been on the news."

I tell Lynne I have to leave for home tonight, a day early, because by tomorrow, Boston flights will be cancelled, and roads will be closed. I can't miss the tests and consultations at Dana-Farber. I am sick to lose a day with Lynne; I walk outside and try to pull myself together and make a plan to leave, but the stress of it all is too much right now. The tears just won't stop.

Then I feel Lynne's arms around me and hear her say, "Mom, it's going to be okay. I'm here. We'll make the new reservations for you. We'll make it easy for you."

Then she says, "The mother on the far right of the welcoming table is a physician. She said what Frank is facing is very serious. If you want to talk with her, she said she would be happy to listen."

After a few deep breaths, I say, "I'm all right. Please thank her for me. I'll just wait out here for a bit."

Lynne waits with me for a few minutes longer, but by then, the musicians are making their way up the stairs to the welcoming table, and I pull in as deep a breath as I can and head back inside.

That evening, I take the red-eye into Boston and meet Frank early morning at the gate. I laugh when he releases Persy's leash so she can run to me, but her little feet move too fast to make traction on the polished floor. By the time we are home, the snow has started and will continue through the night.

By late afternoon the next day, the roads are slick and only partially cleared. It takes two hours to arrive at the Longwood Inn, where Dana-Farber patients receive discounted rates and free parking. The inn faces a busy street, and the hospital is an easy short walk from there. At dinner, Frank has a martini, and I have a glass of merlot. Finally we relax and feel prepared for tomorrow's tests, which start very early, almost before sunrise. It will be a long day.

After dinner, I email Lynne:

> *By the way, there's a piano at Dana-Farber. When there's a player, the music takes us away from our reasons for being here. If there is a cancer center near you that has a piano or place for the girls to perform, please consider the absolute good the music would do for people like us and hundreds of others. Those precious notes waft through the air we are breathing and bring us to another level of hope. I can't explain it; they just do.*

The night is a restless one. We both toss and turn and wait for the morning alarm.

As a nurse, I have always recognized that
every person with a potentially deadly disease
can benefit from the active involvement of a
personal caregiver. Whether the caregivers are
family members or close acquaintances, they
can help bridge the gap between hope and
despair, can help provide clarity in the midst of
confusion, and they can help guide the patient
along a path fraught with fear and anxiety.

—B. Joyce Gilmore, RN (Retd.)[14]

CHAPTER 13

We Are Not Alone

The next day is Valentine's Day. Just before sunrise, we check out of the inn and walk to Dana-Farber. I spend the whole day sitting in one waiting room after another, on one floor and another, while Frank goes through the battery of tests. During one long stretch, a woman wheels in a cart filled with small white gift bags with pink tissue paper popping out the tops. She stops to give a bag to all those with white wristbands, and smiles as she says, "Happy Valentine's Day."

We may think we are alone in this journey through survival mode, but we are not. These little bags of cheer were made by third-grade students from a local school as part of the Friends of Dana-Farber Program. The concern for cancer patients radiates in wide circles. Frank hands the bag to me. I unwrap bits of candy, ChapStick, and a small pad of paper and pencil. It is a long day.

Once home, we study the health care proxy word for word, and I swear to Frank I will honor his wishes, but we have to know what they are. He knows that years ago, I failed my father, who had Parkinson's disease and had asked for no heroic measures. When he was taken to the hospital by ambulance, I was asked if antibiotics should be given, and I said, "Yes." I could not reach my brothers for help in this decision. I wasn't ready to let him die, and I didn't understand that antibiotics were considered "heroic." Shortly after that, Parkinson's disease ravaged his muscles. I felt tremendous guilt. I will not make that mistake again.

"What do you want me to do?" I ask.

"If I have cognitive damage, I do not want to live."

"What does that mean?"

"Just that. I don't want to live."

"So you'll kill yourself?"

"I guess."

"But if your cognitive damage is that advanced, do you think you'll be able to figure out when it's the best time to die?"

"No, and that's why we have to talk about this."

I wait for more instructions.

"The same goes if I am bedridden and completely dependent on others."

"I am not going to kill you," I say. "I think we have to consider assisted suicide."

"Okay. Enough," Frank says. "All this is too hypothetical for me. We need to talk with someone to help us. It's one thing to 'wish' this but another to be within the law, and right now, I don't know what the law is. But there is another big problem, and that's our finances. They could be completely drained keeping me alive if my body won't quit. I won't let that happen to you."

"So what do we do?"

"We've got the realities of cancer and old age compounded by the legalities of the health care proxy and the law. I'm too tired to work this out right now. Let's do it later."

"That's fine with me. It's been a long day."

It's snowing again. I make a quick run to the grocery store, which turns out to be not-so quick because the long checkout line is at a standstill. The delay is caused by a woman wearing a bright-red hat with bows and pom-poms. She leans over the counter to chat with the cashier. The cart behind me hits my ankles. I turn around, and I am met with a scowl. I can feel the tension. Suddenly the woman with the red hat turns to all of us behind her and says, "I'm so sorry, but I had to tell my friend I am cancer-free." People applaud. I study her thin face and wrists and the tufts of hair under her red hat, and instead of thinking the bows and pom-poms are rather funny and overdone, I admire her for taking the time to tell a friend such good news, regardless of those waiting. Maybe I will be that person someday.

Later that day, I receive an email from a friend in New Hampshire who has learned about Frank's cancer. She writes about her church prayer group whose members submit names:

> *We filled out the St. Andrew's Prayer List with Frank's name, describing him as a family friend who was undergoing treatment for cancer. As you can see, this is not a list of people just on a piece of paper but continuous prayers said by parishioners during certain services. There is nothing you have to do. We will monitor Frank's condition with you and make any necessary changes. However, we will keep both of you in our thoughts and prayers. Love to both of you.*

I am overwhelmed by the images of strangers praying for us. A warm rush seems to take hold of me when I read these words. I put my hand over my mouth and hold my breath, imagining the members of the prayer group standing or sitting in a circle, holding hands, eyes closed, and praying for Frank. Complete strangers praying for us. Tears run down my cheeks. I don't stop them. I can't remember ever feeling such compassion from strangers.

When February's calendar is open on my desk, I know we are in a crisis. Frank insists we complete my lessons on the finances with the time that is left, and we do. I fill the freezer with food that will be easy to cook, cross out calendar dates for "Dana-Farber" days, and there's little time for anything else. Family visits more often, friends call more often, unexpected emails from friends and relatives are more frequent. I am losing weight, but food will not settle easily.

Not only do we have to prepare Frank for three weeks in isolation, but we have to prepare the condo for when he returns. His body's ability to fight any infection will be so compromised that we have to protect him from germs, mold, and bacteria. Every room has to be vacuumed and dusted, the rugs must be shampooed, the drapes must be cleaned, and the bathrooms and kitchen must be cleaned thoroughly. For the first month home, the shower, toilet, and sink must be cleaned daily to prevent mold, mildew, fungi, and viruses. Lysol wipes work well. Frank cannot be in a room while it is being cleaned and must wait thirty minutes before returning. Laundry has to be done with warm water; all new clothes have to be washed first, and the same detergent has to be used to prevent rashes. Frank cannot touch any plants because of the possibility of mold. That is just the condo.

Frank has restrictions for his three weeks in isolation: he can bring books, a phone, and a laptop but cannot have nail clippers, deodorant, toothbrush, or toothpaste. The hospital will provide those items. Anything he brings will be wiped with a cleaning solution before they are brought into his room, as will any items I may bring. He should expect what little hair he has to fall out, so the program recommends warm caps, but they have to be washed in warm water first.

If Frank could bring his moccasins from home, he would, but he can't. He needs new ones that have not been touched. We head off to the L.L. Bean store for a new pair. As Frank asks the clerk for a box of moccasins that hasn't been opened, the young clerk says, "Sure," and heads into a back room. When he returns, he opens the box, unravels the tissue paper around each moccasin, and begins to hand Frank the moccasins.

Frank looks at me for help. I can tell he's feeling tired and is reluctant to have to explain that he has cancer, so I step in to explain our situation. Right then, the clerk raises his eyebrows, nods his head, disappears into the back room, and reappears with an unopened box. We buy the moccasins and a new cloth bag to carry Frank's books, computer, and phone. Frank can have his underwear as long as it's been washed in hot water, has gone through the dryer, and is immediately put in a plastic bag.

The only way I can get Frank to write his obituary is to ask that he do it as a favor to me, and I ask matter-of-factly.

"But I don't want an obituary. I've already told you this."

"I know but as a favor to me." The next day, his obituary is on my desk.

The stem cell-transplant process starts on Friday of this week. We are as ready as we know how to be.

I hear from Betty, my fellow trumpet player from band, who lives only a few miles from the hospital. She invites me to stay with her for as long as I would like and gives me my own keys so I can come and go on my own schedule. I am grateful for this friendship. We trumpet players stay together. Over the years, we have come great distances together learning to read music, note by note, then measure by measure. We studied slurs, arpeggios, scales, syncopation, and jazz. We started the I Can't Wait; It's Too Late Club, a bunch of older musicians who met monthly to practice and overcome our dread of being singled out to play before the entire band. After the practices in my living room, we moved to the dining room for potluck dinners. Frank would join us, and we would all talk of theater, music, books, plays, and events in Boston. We began those evenings with racing hearts as we played our solos, and we ended them with laughter and good conversation and the promise to set a date for the next one.

There is power in a caregiver's ability to bear witness to a person who is suffering from serious illness. Being seen and validated in illness can provide strength to a sick person, as they carry that acknowledgment as their ongoing proof of importance in this world. However, bearing witness is so very difficult, and the strength to do so clearly comes from the love shared between a patient and their caregiver.

—Dr. Nancy T. Skehan, MD[15]

CHAPTER 14

Neupogen, Apheresis

As I learned from all the booklets and brochures provided us by the hospital, stem cells in bone marrow make all the body's blood cells: white blood cells that fight infection, red blood cells that carry oxygen, and platelets that help blood to clot. The chemotherapy that Frank will be given in isolation will kill his stem cells, white and red blood cells, and platelets. Because the stem cells are killed, Frank's body will be unable to make white and red blood cells or platelets. This is why Frank's team will harvest his stem cells before he enters isolation, freeze them at the hospital, and reinfuse them when his body is ready. Since there are not enough stem cells in Frank's blood for harvesting, he is given three shots of Newpogen to stimulate the production of stem cells.

On Sunday, I drive Frank to the hospital for the third shot and stay with him as he checks in at a nearby inn. Apheresis, the process of harvesting his stem cells, will begin very early tomorrow morning. I say goodbye and leave for home.

When I arrive at the hospital the next day, Frank is in bed in a large open hospital room filled with equipment, chairs, and personnel. He smiles, and I gently take his hand. Tubes are attached to each arm at the elbow; one tube withdraws blood and sends it to a machine called a cell separator, the size of a small camp-sized refrigerator. The technician sits beside him as the machine accepts his blood from one arm, extracts the stem cells, and returns the blood through a tube attached to the other arm. This takes six to seven hours and will continue tomorrow. The process will not stop until millions of stem cells are collected. Once collected, they will remain frozen until after six days of intense chemotherapy in the stem cell-transplant ward. I stay through lunch and return home, thankful the roads are now clear of snow.

On the third day of apheresis, millions of stems cells have been collected, and the line is flushed. I have a long talk with a nurse about just how gruesome the chemo is during isolation. She says Frank will be tired but not too uncomfortable or too symptomatic for the six days of chemo. She adds that he will have a very hard time during days seven through ten, after the stem cells are reintroduced. Most likely, he will not want any company those days, but after that, he should start to feel better. She speaks with confidence and calm. I pray that he survives and that this is not too hard.

When Frank is dressed and released from the hospital, we drive home but only for two days. He rests and says often how good it is to be home. It is reassuring to have him home and have him near. He's tired and doesn't feel well and lacks an appetite. He tries to rest as much as he can. I stay close.

Betty emails:

> *Am putting a front door key under the flower pot by the front door for you. That way you can come and go as you please. Our hours around here are erratic. Am glad you will bring your cornet. It can be life giving—helps to have something to make the world a more beautiful place, something to join in with other people. Saturday evening we'll have supper here with old friends.*

Kind words can be short and easy to speak,
but their echoes are truly endless.

—Mother Theresa[16]

CHAPTER 15

Red Sweaters for Chickens

March 2017

March 3, 2017: Jeannie and I drive Frank to Dana-Farber for the start of his three weeks in isolation. We park the car, take the elevator to the isolation ward, and walk through two sets of doors. A sign on the doors reminds us to keep them closed because the air is controlled and provides a specialized environment to protect patients from infection. The nurse behind the desk asks us to sign in. Around the periphery of the ward are closed doors that are the patients' rooms. At each door is a metal chest with supplies for the nurses and supplies for us: masks, gloves, wipes, and hand-sanitizing gel. In the center of the ward is a circular counter, behind which are multiple seats and computers for the nurses.

Frank checks in and heads to his room. Jeannie and I stand outside the room next to the table with visitor supplies. We are instructed to wipe our hands with the gel and to put on gloves and a mask if we want to enter the room. Through the door, we see hanging IV bags on portable stands, charts, and computers. We stay in the hallway to say goodbye. Frank comes to me and wraps his arms around me. I feel his breath on my cheek.

"Just come home," I beg. Frank's smile is reassuring, and when he hugs Jeannie, he tells her he has wiped the coin clean. As we leave, I put my arm around Jeannie and whisper, "Thank you." We don't talk much on the way home. I am grateful to have her do the driving and to have her near.

I am seventy-four years old. Years ago, I hadn't thought much about aging and dying, but now I do, especially at night when I can't sleep. No one can convince me a gym membership will help the stiffness in my joints or my concern about falling. It isn't the right time for me to step on a treadmill or work up a sweat on a stationary bike. I don't want any of that. What I do want are safe days where I wake up feeling as good as I did the day before, days when my thoughts are about traveling, visiting museums, taking walks, playing my cornet in band, and making dinner reservations with friends. I want to do all of this with Frank.

Each day of the stem cell transplant is numbered, and that is helpful.

March 4, 2017, chemo day 1: This is the first day of six days of intense chemotherapy to kill cancer cells. I have packed a bag for Betty's and am grateful to have a place close to the hospital at the end of this day. Most of the morning, I answer calls from family and friends and promise to report back. By early afternoon, I return from my walk with Persy, put her in the kitchen with the gate up, and wrap two loaves of freshly baked banana bread, my house gift to my friend, who does not bake. I also pack my cornet and a bottle of wine in case we have a few moments to relax. As I near the hospital parking garage, traffic is stopped in both directions as an ambulance works its way past pedestrians and cars. Drivers are doing their best to allow space for the ambulance, but for some jerks, it's not enough, and they lean on their horns. I sigh in frustration, knowing my time with Frank will be shortened since I want to leave for Betty's before rush hour.

When all is cleared, I drive seven levels down to the first free spot, lock the car, and take the elevator to Frank's floor. The double doors remind me again that the air is controlled on this ward. I wipe my hands with gel, put on a mask and gloves, and enter the room.

Frank is in bed, his head on the pillow, his eyes closed. He is happy to see me and says he feels okay, just tired. I stay for an hour. There is not much to say since the slightest squeeze of his hand on mine is enough. I leave Frank's bedside and promise to return tomorrow.

My GPS takes me the long way to Betty's, through Cambridge and Harvard Square during rush hour, and gives no direction when I come to a fork. I take the wrong fork and arrive much later than I expected but with enough time to play a few trumpet duets, sip some wine, and laugh. Later, Betty, her family, and friends from our I Can't Wait; It's Too Late Club surround the dinner table and fill the evening with light conversation. Tonight I am one of them, moving around in this life just as they are. The evening is such a wonderful break for me that I sleep through the night. By morning, I am hungry and search everywhere for the banana bread. I look in the refrigerator, the freezer, and the kitchen drawers but cannot find it. I leave for home before everyone is up.

Chemo day 2: Persy runs in circles when I open the door, so happy to see me that I have to wonder what goes through her mind when I leave. We take a long walk. Before lunch, I return to the hospital, walk through the double doors, sign in, wipe my hands, and put on a mask and gloves. Frank is tired, but he smiles and asks that I pull the chair closer to him.

"I've been trying to watch a movie," he says, barely above a whisper, "but I lose my concentration."

"One of the *Indiana Jones* movies?"

"Yes. Just can't keep focused."

"Last night at Betty's, everyone asked for you. Wondered how you are doing."

"That's nice." His eyes close. "Did you have fun?"

I can tell it's an effort for him to make conversation, even light conversation.

"We did have fun. Laughed and told stories."

"That's nice." He's drifting off.

Just then, a nurse enters, asks Frank how he is doing, writes something on the large blackboard on the wall opposite his bed, and leaves. Shortly after that, there's another knock, and his lunch is delivered.

"I think I should leave, let you rest and have your lunch. I'll go to the cafeteria for something to eat."

All the cafeteria seats are taken, so I search for a quiet place to eat my sandwich. Around the corner is a small room with a sofa. I sit there alone, unaware of the time passing. I am happy to be away by myself and from the sounds of doors opening and closing, feet shuffling along the floor, and quiet conversations not meant for me to hear. It's a respite, if only for a short time, before I return to Frank's room.

"Will I see you tomorrow?" Frank asks.

"Yes, I'll come by at lunchtime. You should rest now."

When I arrive home, I call to thank Betty and ask where the banana bread went. She laughs. "Uh-oh, I hid them so I could bring them as a house gift this evening. They were too beautiful for us to eat. So sorry you didn't get a chance to find any, but your bread is better than anything I would make."

Chemo day 3: Traffic is jammed on my way into Boston. There was an accident, and drivers are slowing down as they pass the crumpled cars. I finally reach the hospital and Frank's ward. After I finish sanitizing my hands and putting on gloves and a mask, I open the door to Frank's room and see him resting.

"Traffic was awful. Sorry I'm late."

"Thought you'd be here sooner. Just glad you're here now," is all he says, and he closes his eyes and reaches for my hand. It's quiet.

"Have you been watching any movies?" I ask. He gently moves his head from side to side. I'm trying to make conversation, but it is hard knowing he may not want to talk. For now, I think my presence is enough. I start to relax. I look around the room. There's an array of medical equipment attached to the arms of a portable stand beside Frank's bed. There are two IV bags of clear fluid and one IV bag that looks like blood. They have dangling tubes, some of which are attached to Frank's arm. There are three small pieces of equipment the size of handheld phones and an array of lines plugged into the wall. Across the room is a large blackboard that lists the names of

Frank's nurses and a chart of his progress, with symbols that mean little to me. His bed is on wheels so they can transport him quickly. Behind me is a computer on a tall stand. Then I look at Frank, resting quietly on his back, his head on his pillow, as though he does not have the strength to raise himself to read or watch a video on his computer. His eyes are closed. I take in a breath as fully as I can and let it out slowly, one after another, until my heart stops racing.

Ginni, my knitting friend, will be coming for dinner tonight. Though it will be a long day in Boston, it will be calming to be around her. She has agreed to take Limerick, the betta fish Alex gave me, for a while and promises to keep her cats from eating it.

Chemo day 4: Outside Frank's room, I rub my hands with gel, put on a mask and gloves, and immediately see that Frank does not feel well. He hoped he could eat his breakfast, but could not, and did not feel well enough to shower. He says his blood pressure is rising, which he thinks may be from the chemicals but may also be from nearly overwhelming anxiety. This is the first time he has mentioned anxiety or blood pressure or that he might die within days. I bite my lip and try to keep thoughts of his death from my mind, but as I look at the outline of his body under the sheet and watch his chest slowly rise and fall, it seems possible he may not come home. His hands are clasped over his chest. He has not reached out to hold my hand since I arrived. His computer and books are neatly arranged on the bedside table, untouched; his slippers are beside his bed, neatly together, just as they are at home. His face is calm. He is not in pain now. If only I could see the start of a smile, I might see hope, but I don't. The room starts to feel too warm. My heart starts to race, and my breathing is shallow. I feel a terror I have not felt before. I wish I had someone's arms to fall into, someone to cradle me and tell me Frank will survive. I reach for some tissues; I am about to sob.

Just then, there is a slight knock on the door. A man with a mask and gloves enters carrying a lunch tray, puts it on the table over the bed, and leaves.

"Frank, your lunch is here," I say in a whisper. I don't want to disturb him, but I know he did not eat his breakfast. "Do you want me to help you?"

"No. I can't eat it now. I'll try later." I can barely make out what he is saying.

"Why don't you sleep now. I'll go to the cafeteria for lunch and come right back."

"Can't you eat here with me?" His voice is barely above a whisper.

"No, I'm not allowed to have food in your room."

"Wake me when you get back if I am asleep, please. I need to know you are here."

The cafeteria is packed, as it always is, and I walk aisle after aisle to find an available seat. Perhaps it's the crowded cafeteria, not knowing anyone, and eating alone that are unpleasant reminders of earlier vagabond years. I start to eat the salad but forgot to get dressing, so I put it aside and eat the sandwich I brought from home.

When I return to Frank's room, he opens his eyes.

"Are you feeling better? I see you ate some of your lunch."

"A little."

"Do you remember when you called me a vagabond?"

"I do. Why?" He turns his head to look at me.

"Look at us now," I say. "Perfectly settled in the condo with no intention of ever moving again. Those days are over." He takes my hand, slowly draws it to his cheek. I think he is drifting off, but as I slowly withdraw my hand, his grip tightens slightly, and I close my eyes, praying he survives.

Chemo day 5: I visit Frank, but he is too tired to talk. Again, I leave for the cafeteria and return to find him asleep. Sitting beside him, holding his hand, I know that our years together have been good. He made sure we had financial security and the peace that comes with that, and though he had only a brother for his family, he had my family and was welcomed into it. Whatever roots we put down, we put down together, as solid and sure as our vow, "till death do us part." When I wake him to say goodbye and to tell him I will not be in tomorrow, he whispers, "That's okay."

Chemo day 6: I want to spend the next three days by Frank's side when the stem cells are introduced, so I take Persy to my brother's house, where she'll be loved for as long as I need. Dropping Persy off takes most of the day.

Day 7, stem cells returned: Today is an important day—Frank's stem cells will be returned, and the start of the worst of this process will begin. However, there is another major snowstorm, and I have to stay home. I am barely able to eat and am so very sorry I am not with Frank that I am on the verge of tears all day. I hope no one calls or comes to the condo. The slightest sign of compassion will make me break down. I drink more water and practice my cornet for as long as I can concentrate. I start reading a book written by a cancer patient who keeps mentioning "being in the moment," but I don't understand what that means, and stop reading. I wish this day would pass.

When the road is plowed, I drive to the grocery store where a wave of unreality washes over me, like breathing in someone's smoke, and you can't see who's smoking. The shredded wheat seems out of place, the aisles and clerks unfamiliar. I'm afraid to turn my head quickly for fear of passing out. My ears fill with white noise. I can't stop these short quick breaths. I hope I remember where I parked my car. I want to go home. I leave the cart midaisle and walk out into the cold. I open my car door, slide in, open the window, and put my forehead on the cold steering wheel until my breathing slows, and I begin to feel my shoulders relax. Finally I look up and find the world just as I had left it: cars still parked in the lot, shoppers unloading their carts, mounds of snow pushed to the side of the parking lot. Whatever came over me has passed, and I leave for home, sorry Persy is with my brother. That night I email Frank to say good night and let him know I will be in tomorrow. I don't mention the episode in the grocery store.

Day 8: I go to the hospital, rub my hands with gel, put on the mask and gloves. The room smells awful, like rotted garlic. It is difficult to keep breathing in that smell. The nurse says the odor is from the solution the returning stem cells were in.

"Can you smell that?" I ask Frank.

But Frank shakes his head slowly and says he can't smell it anymore. He feels nauseous and weak. This is the day after his stem cells were returned. Nearly every morning, he showers and shaves, and I wonder why he would do that when he feels so weak. He tells me that if he cleans up before the doctors arrive on their rounds, they will know he takes care of himself. He expects the doctors to do the same for him. His head rests on two pillows, his eyes stay closed, and when I say I should leave so he can rest, he says, "No, please stay. We don't need to talk, but if I fall asleep, wake me and let me know you're leaving."

Day 9: I return to Dana-Farber. This is the third day after the transplant. Frank is weak, tired, and just too sick to do anything but hold my hand and ask about Persy.

"She's fine," I tell him. "She'll be at my brother's for a bit. I miss her snuggling next to me at night." I wipe the tears running down his cheek. He is too weak to reach for the tissues. He has lost all his hair.

When his lunch is brought in, I leave for the cafeteria, but again all the tables are taken. I walk up one aisle and down another, but there are no seats. I ask a woman if I may join her. When she asks why I am at the hospital, tears bubble up.

"That's okay," she says and reaches across the table for my hand.

"Everything about me has turned inside out or wrong side in or twisted out of shape," I tell her.

She nods. "It's like being on a train, isn't it, looking out the window and not recognizing shapes or people or languages, or anything familiar, and you don't know where you're going."

"Yes."

"For nearly five years, my sister went through leukemia treatment. I cared for her. I understand."

"I am struck by the others here," I say, "especially those with sick children or the older couples, and wonder how they cope." My sandwich is untouched. We are quiet for a moment.

"I have a friend, Ginni," I say, "who knits knitted knockers as bra fillers for women who have had mastectomies. She's doing her bit to help. When this is over, I'll find my way to help."

My lunch mate adds with a touch of excitement, "My friend is a knitter too. As a matter of fact, she had a fashion show on YouTube."

"Wow, a fashion show? For what?"

"For her chickens."

I lean a bit forward and say, "What?"

"Her chickens are from the south, where the weather is warm!"

"What does she knit for them?"

"Red sweaters."

"Sweaters for what?"

"The chickens."

"For what?"

"To keep them warm up here in the north."

"How do you put a sweater on a chicken?"

"I don't know, but she knits them, dresses them up, and has a fashion show with other chicken sweater knitters."

"Chicken sweater knitters," I repeat as laughter rises from my gut into my mouth like fizz from champagne.

My lunch mate stands, picks up her tray, and says, "Hey, check it out on YouTube." I'm still smiling as I slowly eat my sandwich, sitting at the table alone. I think about chickens with red sweaters over their wings, strutting across some runway. After lunch, I return to Frank's room where he is just as I left him. He didn't eat his food, and his eyes are closed. His smile is faint when I relate the red sweaters for chickens story, but it is a smile nevertheless. He takes my hand and says he needs to sleep, that I can leave for home.

This lunch is a turning point for me. The laugh that pushed its way up into my throat felt good. I remember looking at this woman who was the caregiver for someone she loved for nearly five years, and I thought, *That is me now.* She smiled when she told me about the red sweaters as if it were a funny thing that happened on her way to work. Maybe I'll be as relieved of this darkness as she seems to be. Maybe not tomorrow, but soon. What a gift she gave me. I never expected her story of caregiving nor did I expect to feel better after telling her that everything inside me was twisted out of shape.

At home later that day, I searched YouTube, and sure enough, there were sweater-wearing chickens being hugged by the chicken-sweater knitters. The knitters proudly put the sweaters on the chickens, and the chickens proudly strutted their handmade sweaters, though I didn't see a runway. It brought me a smile again.

Something changes in me. Now instead of holding back the truth about how I feel, I tell whoever asks that I am scared and upset and that I hope these feelings will pass. I also say, "No thanks. I don't need you to come over. I'm really okay. This is just how it is right now."

Day 10: I return to the hospital. Frank is still weak. I leave shortly after arriving to have lunch in the cafeteria. As I'm heading for the elevator, I notice a woman I had seen earlier. "I saw you the other day at the elevator. How are you doing?"

"Okay," she says bravely.

"Me too," I say. "Is your husband in ward B?" This is where Frank is.

"No, ward A. He's in day 10 and is so sick. The nausea is horrible. I can hardly stand to see him this way."

Our hands reach out and touch lightly. The elevator opens, and our conversation ends until I meet her again at the cafeteria. We find a table that has two chairs, not an easy task at lunchtime. She tells me it all started when her husband had a mild heart attack. While the doctors took care of that, they found cancer.

"We were scared when he had the heart attack," she says, "but now I'm thinking it may have saved his life. That is, if he survives this transplant."

"We have a big month ahead of us when they come home," I say. "Did you have to get all your rugs cleaned?"

"No, we've all hardwood floors and no curtains."

"No curtains?"

"We live in a rural area, but we have to wipe down all the wood, ceiling to floor. I have friends to help. It's taking days."

That is the last time I see her, but it feels good to have talked with someone who is going through what I am. I'm sorry her husband has the extreme vomiting. I know some of the patients in Frank's ward are wracked by vomiting, too, because I can hear them. So far Frank has escaped this. I hope he continues to do so.

Day 11: Another blizzard, and I stay home.

Day 12: When I arrive to see Frank, his lunch is on the tray. I tell him I'll be back after lunch in the cafeteria. I grab a sandwich and look for a place to sit, but all the seats are taken until I reach the far end where an older man is seated, his head cradled on his arms on the table, asleep. He wears winter boots, and on the floor by his feet is a heavy winter jacket and a stuffed shopping bag. I imagine he has a long commute to visit a patient and is exhausted. Silently I wish him and the patient he is here to see better days.

Day 13: I wipe my hands with gel outside Frank's door and put on a mask and gloves. Frank is still weak and nauseous and so tired his eyelids droop. I offer to leave, but he takes my hand and says no, he will sleep after I leave. We stay like that for a while.

"It feels good to have you here," he whispers.

I walk out into the pod, the area outside the patients' rooms. The nurses don't look up from their work. I suspect they have ears like a mother who doesn't have to see the child to know every creak, cough, or silence when there shouldn't be. I see a thin man, possibly in his forties or early fifties. His mask covers half his face, and his eyes never look at me as he swings his gloved hands with each step, going from one end of the pod to the other. The distance is little more than half a circle, maybe twenty steps, and then he turns around, retraces his steps, and continues back and forth. When he can, Frank also exercises in the pod, attached to his pole with IV bags, but it is exhausting.

Day 14: I stay home to rewash T-shirts and underpants in hot water, put them in the dryer, and immediately fold them into a plastic bag. Before dinner, I call Frank on the phone. I expect a short conversation. Instead, he sounds almost normal, saying he's been watching an *Indiana Jones* video, the one with all the rats. His voice is stronger than it has been in days.

"Oh god, that was awful when they were underground in water with the rats swimming around."

"Did you know the movie producers had those rats bred specially for that film? They bred them not to bite the actors."

"Still it makes me squirm just to think about them."

"Here's the funny part," Frank continues, "the movie companies always purchase insurance to protect themselves against production delays, but here the movie company was concerned about something happening to those specially bred rats, so they took out insurance on the rats, and the insurer insisted on a thousand-rat deductible."

We both laugh.

"You must be feeling better. This is the most you've spoken in fourteen days."

"I am. I think we've rounded a corner."

"Keep doing what you're doing, and you'll be home soon."

Day 15: I have the condo ducts professionally cleaned and sanitized.

Day 16: I arrive at the hospital just before lunch, put on a mask and gloves, and clean the plastic bag of T-shirts and underpants with disinfecting wipes. Frank is sitting on a chair by his bed. He smiles.

"Wow," I say. "You're sitting up."

"My blood levels are rising, everyone is happy. I'm going to make it. I even finished the movie."

"A few more days," I say gently.

There is a slight knock on the door. Lunch arrives. Frank's face says it all when he takes the top off of the grilled cheese sandwich, which is partially browned, partially warm, and has partially melted cheese on airy white bread. No hot cheese oozing out the sides of a perfectly grilled sandwich, begging to be eaten. He looks over at me and says, "See, this is what isolation is like. I'm craving a Reuben sandwich. Do you think there's some way to make that work at home? Can you get wrapped pastrami at the supermarket, something no one has touched? I'd love a tomato on this grilled cheese, but I know I can't have that. And while you're at it, how about some fresh fruit. I can have thick-skinned fruit, like oranges, avocados, melon, but no strawberries, blueberries, or grapes."

His appetite is returning right on time, and he is thinking about coming home. Mercifully we have turned this corner.

After nineteen days in isolation, Frank can come home but not before hours of consultations with the doctors and nutritionists. Before I leave the house on his release day, I disinfect everything in the kitchen I think Frank may touch: light switches, refrigerator handle, cupboard knobs, microwave, and every part of the sink and counter. I do the same in the bathrooms, the bedroom and dining room, and then the doorknobs, inside and outside. I repeat the process with every surface of the car, inside and out.

On my way into Boston, I feel on edge about Frank coming home. He's been in someone else's care for nearly three weeks, and now he will be in mine. I think I have everything prepared and cleaned, but I second-guess myself. I'm distracted and start driving into the parking garage in the wrong lane. I catch my mistake and back out as cars in either direction stop and wait. I shake my head and sigh, pull my shoulders back, and try again.

For the last time, I wipe down all the bags with alcohol wipes, put my vest under the nurses' counter, and see Frank through the window door, sitting quietly, bald, waiting. For the last time, I wipe my hands with gel, put on gloves and mask, and go in. He is dressed in a button-down shirt, jeans, wool socks, and moccasins. He stands by his bed, smiling.

Providing care does not end at feeding, dressing, tending to wounds, or palliating pain; it is an all-encompassing act of endorsement of a patient's desire to live.

—Dr. Nancy T. Skehan, MD[17]

CHAPTER 16

I Am His Protector

I am Frank's protector, making meals, washing clothes, wiping toilets, light switches, doorknobs, and countertops with disinfectants, picking up medicines, buying cotton caps and soft toilet paper, shopping for the foods he can eat, and cleaning out any foods he can't. I bake bread and make macaroni and cheese, knowing he may only pick at them, replace emptied bottles of hand sanitizers, and monitor him so I have notes to share with Dr. J.

Frank's immune system is very weak. Even a cold could be deadly at this point. He has to be protected from bacteria, viruses, mold, and airborne germs, and he simply cannot get sick. For at least a month, I can't use wooden spoons in the kitchen because they may harbor bacteria and mold; all our clothes must be washed in hot water, and all guests must wear gloves and a mask. Persy cannot sleep with us, though this rule will be hard to follow, especially for Frank. He cannot have pepper because it is raw. Anything from the deli or anything that someone has touched is forbidden. No salads. No fruit unless it has thick skin and is washed well. Nothing from the bakery. He can leave the house but must wear a mask and gloves, and cannot be in contact with people.

As we leave the hospital, carrying only a small bag of T-shirts, underpants, computer, and books, we look at each other and smile. Nothing needs to be said.

Ten miles from Boston, Frank starts crying and says, "I am so grateful for all you've done." In bed that night, he sobs again.

Tonight I am not crying. Frank is home.

On Frank's third day home from the hospital, he chauffeurs me to the post office and grocery store and stays in the Jeep. He wears his hospital gloves and mask, wipes down the inside of the Jeep with Clorox wipes, and takes a nap.

We now take Persy for a walk two times a day together, which is a quarter of a mile each time, but it is a start. We increase the speed and distance each day. Often for lunch, we have grilled cheese sandwiches with cheese oozing out the sides and the bread grilled to perfection. He eats honeydew melons and navel oranges. It will be weeks or months before he can have strawberries, blueberries, or grapes, but that is okay; we do fine with thick-skinned fruit.

Some days he is cold and unable to get warm even with the condo thermostat set at seventy-six degrees. A rice bag heated in the microwave does little to help warm his hands. Despite this, his temperature is normal, and that's good. I'm sweating in my T-shirt.

Though he is diligent about caring for his teeth and mouth, Frank's gums start to be a problem. We were told to expect this from the chemotherapy, but a sore mouth will be a problem if it gets worse and becomes painful enough to cause trouble eating. Once his white blood cell count recovers, this problem should go away. He still isn't allowed to floss.

His hearing is worse, which is a side effect of the chemotherapy. Hearing aids are at the top of my list to talk about, but not right now. Some days he doesn't look right, and I know he does not feel well and is tired, nauseous and achy. Maybe it is because he overdid it the day before; I must remember to tell the doctor.

After five days home, we are back at the hospital for blood work and an appointment with Dr. J. The best part is knowing it is only a temporary visit. Frank wears his gloves and mask, like many others here. The blood draw waiting room is packed with hardly a spare seat, let alone two together. We find two seats in the corridor, but Frank will not be able to hear his name called from that distance. I might not hear it either, so I stand near the front of the room. When I look back, Frank is slouched in his chair, his head drooped, his eyes closed, no different than most here who are wearing a mask. I wonder how this blood draw room can be so packed every time we come. It doesn't seem to matter the day or the time.

Frank's name is called. The nurse greets him with a smile, checks his white bracelet, and leads him behind the door. Five minutes later, he returns with a blue band around his elbow area. He walks slowly and nods to me that we can leave for the cafeteria. I hold his arm as we exit the elevator and walk to the coffee machines. He barely touches the coffee. There is little he can eat here, as most of the food is a salad bar open to the public, or in steaming trays behind the counters. I offer him a sandwich I brought, but he shakes his head. The clock seems to barely move as we wait to see Dr. J.

We have good news: Frank's progress is normal. The blood counts are where they should be. As we return to the elevator, I overhear two men in wheelchairs say their cancers have come back. My back stiffens, and I remind myself to focus only on us right now. Maybe this is what "being in the moment" means.

On March 30, 2017, seven days after returning home from the stem cell transplant, Frank has a setback. He feels nauseous and has little energy. He will eat my homemade chicken soup with vegetables but only a cup instead of a bowl. Midafternoon, I bring him a tray of toast, tea, and scrambled eggs. He eats it all and says he is feeling better. By late afternoon, he is well enough to walk with Persy and me.

"Could you do me a favor?" he asks. "I ordered corned beef and cabbage in the hospital, but by the time dinner was served, the kitchen ran out of it."

"Are you sure your stomach is ready for that?"

"No, but let's try it."

I know he won't eat it, but tomorrow, I'll cook it anyway. Another nor'easter with high winds will dump a foot of snow, and we'll be housebound until the streets are plowed, and we are shoveled out.

The clock says 2:00 a.m. I'm wide awake. I walk to the kitchen, put on some water for tea, and pull back the shutters to see the first of the snowflakes caught on the leafless tree branches. The road is still bare, but that will not be the case in a few hours. The air is so still my eyes catch a single snowflake from above, and I watch it slowly drop. It won't be long before the wind will push the snow sideways, making it impossible to see beyond the trees in our tiny front yard. But right now, as I watch the snow slowly fall, I feel the quiet and peace as clearly as if I were outside standing under the tree limb catching the first snowflakes.

Morning is bright, almost blinding white, with the sun on the new snow. By afternoon, our driveway is plowed, our sidewalk is shoveled, and right now, everything about the condo is perfect: sunlight pours in on three sides, a tap on the thermostat raises the temperature, we have plenty of food, everything is on one floor. I do a quick grocery run for corned beef and cabbage, and the store is nearly empty.

All afternoon, Frank is too tired to go for a walk, and by dinnertime, he leans his elbows on the table and cups his chin in his hands. He pushes the corn beef and cabbage around the plate and finally says, "I'm sorry." So I cook fried eggs and toast. He eats it all. It is a struggle to figure out what healthy foods he will eat. He won't touch asparagus, broccoli, and spinach nor will he eat red meat. Chicken soup seems a winner, but he doesn't want that every day. I'm reminded of Dr. A. suggesting Chubby Hubby to keep the calories high. I'll make pea soup and homemade biscuits tomorrow.

He has lost ten pounds since coming home. The hardest is seeing him so fragile. He is bald, weak, hunched over, and wrapped up in a wool blanket. This is expected, I know. Persy spends most of her time snuggled on Frank's lap, not moving until Frank stirs. I hope tomorrow is better.

The tomorrows do get better. The progress is slow, but it is progress. Frank eats more, gets out of his chair more, and we walk longer, even in the cold. He is happy to chauffeur me to the store and pharmacy, which is the extent of his stamina right now.

Such short little lives our pets have to
spend with us, and they spend most of it
waiting for us to come home each day.

—John Grogan, *Marley & Me: Life and Love with the World's Worst Dog*[18]

CHAPTER 17

A Punch in the Gut

Spring 2017

April brings changes. I have more energy and am putting on some of the weight I lost. I will resume art classes, cornet lessons, and band. The smell of spring filters in through the kitchen window and front door, bringing with it air that wipes clean winter's gloom. Soon the bulbs I planted in the fall will pop through, and the planters on the porch deck will be ready for flowers.

Frank's blood work and tests in Boston are routine and easy to schedule. These are big steps and reassuring ones. A PET scan in June, two months away, is the next hurdle. If it shows the diffuse large B-cell cancer is in remission, it will be good news. If a PET scan two years after that shows the same, then the diffuse large B-cell cancer is considered cured. The risk of a recurrence after two years is very low. Still, the follicular lymphoma is a chronic incurable disease.

In a couple months, Frank plans to play golf even if he has to rest in the cart for most holes. He can now take day trips to take pictures, which was impossible until recently. A good friend will fly to Louisiana, pick up the RV from the storage barn, and drive it here by the first of May. Traveling to the West Coast in the RV is still our plan, but this summer, our travels in the RV will be closer to home, just a few days at a time.

As we drive to Boston this second week in April, the mask and gloves are on the dashboard of the Jeep, and Frank will only wear them in the hospital now. The doctor tells us Frank can have salads, but none from an open salad bar. Frank's bone marrow is functioning as expected. His immune system is recovering. Four blood levels look normal, but two are not, and that is to be expected at this stage. Frank's continued nausea is a concern, so Dr. J. orders a different medicine. He still needs to avoid crowds, stores, or restaurants. Lettuce, tomatoes, cukes, and peppers are on the shopping list now. He can't have moldy cheeses yet, but that is okay. I still make all of our bread.

Our days are passing with a new normalcy until a mast cell tumor, a form of cancer, is discovered on Persy's back at a routine veterinarian exam. It has characteristics similar to Frank's lymphoma—it may or may not grow larger or may transform into another kind of cancer. I cannot hold back a heavy sigh or the urge to cry; it does not seem possible that this little nine pounds of love has cancer. I allow them to draw blood and take a biopsy of the tumor, and I schedule an appointment to do the ultrasound to see if it has spread to her lymph nodes. She's only five years old, for heaven's sake. If we don't do anything, she may have six months. Please, I don't want any more news like these.

By the third week of April, we are buoyed by longer days and warming afternoons. I till the ground for a garden in Jeannie's backyard and can actually feel my smile; the more dirt I turn, the happier I am. My bucket is full of trowels, worm castings, and seeds.

We return to Dana-Farber. Most restrictions are removed, except for close contact with people at restaurants and theaters. We are nearly through this.

At the end of the month, the vet tells us Persy's ultrasound showed nothing abnormal internally. The cancer will be removed next week. Until then, Persy acts and looks like nothing is wrong. I am reminded of the long corridor we first walked down on the oncology wing. Who would have known Frank had cancer by looking at him then? It's the same with Persy.

Frank and I drive Persy to the animal hospital for surgery. Frank waits in the Jeep as I take her in. I wrap her in my arms, check in at the desk, and wait for the assistant to come for her. She sits quietly with her head resting on my knees, and I can feel her little heart beating against my legs. As other dogs walk by us, she does not move; her tiny paws seem to cling to my legs. The assistant reaches for her and walks away, with Persy looking over her shoulder back at me. I turn away and head home. The operation goes well.

Toward the end of May, two months after leaving the isolation ward, Frank's blood work results show he is doing well, but he is not fully recovered. He can shop in grocery stores and eat in restaurants now, but he cannot eat any foods from a salad bar or, for a year, food that has been kept hot in a steamer nor can he do any gardening because of the risk of mold. None of this is bothersome.

Persy is back to normal, barking at the UPS truck and strangers, careening around corners with excitement, and making sure she has plenty of time on Frank's lap. My garden at Jeannie's is bursting with tomatoes, beans, cukes, and zucchini, and I love sharing them with my new condo friends. The days are hot. We make reservations at a campground in the Berkshire Mountains in western Massachusetts for three days in July. The camper is in fine shape, all the gear we need is stored just as we left it in Louisiana, and our clothes are neatly folded in the closets. All we have to do is pack food. Ginni and I go to movies on rainy afternoons, and I visit with Jeannie. We are happy to be returning to the things we love doing. We have crossed the bridge and choose not to look back.

PART 3

TAPS AND STEADY FOOTING

In many cases, the caregiver is the one person who knows everything that is going on with the patient.

—*American Cancer Society Handbook*[19]

CHAPTER 18

The News Is Not Good

June 2017

Finally it is June, the day for Frank's first PET scan since the stem cell transplant. It will tell us if the cancer is in remission, which we certainly expect it to be. To celebrate, we make reservations for this evening at our favorite Boston restaurant, Atlantic Seafood. We already know our orders: swordfish and salmon. We have talked about this dinner for weeks, but first Frank has to have the test, and we have to meet with Dr. J.

It takes about an hour for Frank to drink the fluid, then another half hour to have the scan. When Frank reappears after the scan, we sit for a moment to gather up our bags. Frank takes my shoulders and sighs deeply. "After this is over, let's walk to Newbury Street, look at the shops, and if it's early enough, I'll buy you a cup of coffee. We'll sit and watch the people. Sound good?"

I lean into his chest and say, "Sounds perfect."

"Best part of today will be dinner at Atlantic Seafood," he says. "We can sit there, relax, have a drink. I'll hold your hand, and we won't need to think about this place." We leave for the eighth floor, the lymphoma floor, and our meeting with Dr. J.

The news is not good. A new tumor has grown on Frank's kidney, which looks like diffuse large B-cell cancer, and it is in a difficult position to biopsy. There is another spot near the center of his belly, which is not as great a concern as the one on his kidney. We need a biopsy to find out what is on his kidney. We hope that after the radiologist reviews the PET scan, he will be willing to do the biopsy, but the placement of the tumor is problematic, and he may not agree to do it. If that's the case, Dr. J. will contact a surgeon, but he is less than encouraging that a surgeon would be willing to try to reach it.

If we decide to do nothing, Frank's prognosis is six months to a year. If the cancer is follicular lymphoma, then there could be additional chemo, which is the best case right now after all his body has been through. If it is diffuse large B-cell cancer, there are other treatments: possibly genetically engineered stem cells, a different chemo, or other treatments that are harsh and may put Frank in a coma for two weeks. This is so hard to grasp. I look at Dr. J. I have nothing to say right now, no comments, no questions. All the excitement for dinner together is gone, and I can hardly breathe.

I bravely tell Dr. J., just above a whisper, "Well, we *were* going to have a celebratory dinner this evening." *Celebratory?* I never use that word. It just popped out. No one smiled.

Dinner is not "celebratory." We cancel the reservations, drive straight home, and agree to sell the camper.

Frank is having the biopsy on the new tumor on his kidney, which will take most of the day. They will not biopsy the new tumor in the middle of his belly, which is too small, according to Dr. J. In about a week, we'll have the results. For most of this day, I sit in an attractive quiet room, watching others come and go. I feel glum and knotted inside. Frank and I never revisited our health care proxy. We should have, I know, but we didn't. Working out details associated with cognitive damage and complete dependency on others was too difficult, and it was far easier for us to ignore them.

Once we find out the results of this biopsy, we are hopeful Dr. J. will recommend a new chemotherapy. The other alternatives are unacceptable. It's this knowledge that alerts me to revisit the health care proxy, but I'm back in the same quandary with the same questions. We will have to deal with this burden later. There are just too many issues to resolve without professional guidance.

I don't have that feeling of *Ah, I bet we beat cancer this time! Let's celebrate*, or *I'm sure we are through driving to Boston and worrying every time we sit in one of the waiting rooms*. Instead, I wait for the new results and brace for any outcome knowing that we have done the best we can.

Meanwhile, we clean out the camper to sell it. My garden at Jeannie's is overflowing with vegetables. My new cornet teacher is working with me with a patience I am grateful for and accepts that I am unable to do all the practicing we both would like. But that is how it is right now, lesson by lesson.

Mid-July, we are back at the hospital, waiting for the doctor to arrive to give us the biopsy results. We cross our legs and fold our arms, and both feel the air, heavy and foreboding. It is an awful feeling. Dr. J. arrives and tells us the biopsy showed no cancer. Both cancers are in remission now. We hardly breathe as we look at each other. Neither of us can speak, so Dr. J. does it for us.

"Well, you two"—he smiles—"go have your celebratory dinner this evening!" We barely return the smile, look at each other, and hear the words, "Your cancer is in remission." The next CT scan is scheduled for six weeks, in August.

I feel the same as Frank, that the cancer may return, but however the next CT scan goes, I hope I am now strong and knowledgeable enough to withstand a setback. The large B-cell cancer is supposedly cured, but it can reoccur. The follicular cancer is not curable. So as I see it, now that both are in remission, I put them behind me. I plan my tomorrows to be full of family and friends, painting, music, and spending as much time outside as possible gardening, walking, and sitting on our tiny deck, breathing in fresh air and watching the chipmunks scamper. I write Betty to tell her I will be back at band for the fall semester, and I sign up for a full semester of cornet lessons, no longer lesson by lesson. I call family and friends to tell the good news.

Summer radiates with sun, the green of trees, the color of flowers. Days are filled with golf, music, vegetable gardening, and long stretches outside walking or sitting on our tiny condo deck. We keep the doors and windows open, as if we are airing ourselves out as well as bringing fresh air into the condo. The August CT scan shows all cancer in remission.

The bond with a dog is as lasting as
the ties of this earth can ever be.

—Konrad Lorenz[20]

CHAPTER 19

Taps

But something is not right with Persy. Frank calls my cell phone as I am driving home from lunch with Jeannie. He is more distraught than I have ever heard him.

"I was walking Persy," he stutters almost uncontrollably, "and she started shaking and then collapsed. I think she had a seizure. A nurse in one of the condos saw us, rushed out, and drove us home."

I arrive home. Frank is visibly shaken. He pats Persy nervously and asks what we should do. Persy looks fine. Whatever it was, it seems to have passed, but not for long. After the next seizure, the vet puts her on medicine, but the seizures continue.

Persy was the joy, the childlike energy that absorbed so much of our stress. To have her greet us after all those trips to the hospital with overwhelming love and to feel her cuddled next to us in bed felt like a tangible shield from the dark.

On the winter solstice of 2018, Persy died. We couldn't control the epilepsy. Frank was with her when she fell to the ground, lifeless. He knew something was wrong because she would never choose to touch water with her tiny feet if she could help it, yet she fell into a shallow puddle by our front steps. He picked her up, brought her to the kitchen, laid her on a fresh towel, and knelt by her, crying. We brought her to the vet, where they prepared a fleece blanket for her. For a long time, we stayed with her, patting her little head, and praying she find a place of peace. For days we felt her nearby, silently craving to have her return. We missed her terribly.

Betty, my trumpet friend, sent a card with a drawing of a trumpet player, and inside she wrote, "Playing taps for Persy—trying to make it beautiful. How beautiful Persy was in her devotion and faithfulness to you. There's an empty space in your hearts tonight."

In January of 2019, two years after the stem cell transplant and nearly five years after I first saw the lump on Frank's neck during *Uncle Vanya,* we are once again in Dr. J.'s office. He tells us all the blood work is normal for this stage of recovery. Our sighs are audible, deep and slow. Ever cognizant of our feelings, Dr. J. waits for us to gather composure. I think he may be waiting for a smile, but I don't feel like smiling; I am much too humbled and thankful.

Instead of heading straight home, we stop in the hospital cafeteria for a bite and find a table in a far corner. There, a few tables from us, is the same woman who held my hand and told me about the red sweaters for chickens. I want to walk over to her and tell her we made it through and how her story of red sweaters for chickens stayed with me and buoyed me. I want her to know that her smile and laughter were sure signs for me that I, too, would find a time to laugh and perhaps pass her story on to others. But when I again look up, she is gone. I leave my table and walk to the corridor, trying to find her by the elevators, but I don't see her.

We continue as is, but we are always aware of what we went through, like a spot on the lens of eyeglasses that cannot be wiped off but is not blurry enough to dull vision. We are so fortunate to be able to look ahead. As the months pass, Frank drives to the grocery store with his dashboard free of gloves and masks, and we both walk the aisles, taking turns pushing the cart and gathering fresh produce, some with thick skins, some not. We travel to Boston for dinner at our favorite restaurant and order our meal, no longer thinking about our aborted celebratory dinner. For my two-hour rehearsal at band, I can relax with my friends, play the parts of the music I can read, and know that when I am through, Frank is waiting for me to drive me home. Friends and relatives meet us at the condo for lunch or dinner. It has been a while since that was possible, but it is now.

Frank, hoping to have his photography exhibited, applied to the Copley Society in Boston, The Providence Art Club in Rhode Island, and to the Salmagundi Club in Manhattan. After passing rigorous juried processes, he was accepted to artistic membership in all three. His photographs continue to be exhibited periodically in those locations. They have also been chosen for marketing brochures, and they have won awards. I design and sew colorful batik book bags for the caregivers I know, attaching one of my watercolor notecards with these words: "I make these bags for the caregivers I know to wish them well and those they care for," and send them off, hoping they brighten someone's day, and to let them know they are not alone.

AFTERWORD

Written by Frank Bartucca

Even though I almost died from it, I know very little about cancer. When mine was first diagnosed, I was not given any treatment. It was a form of cancer which can remain nonthreatening for many years and is treated only if and when it spreads and becomes aggressive. For me, this period of grace lasted about two years. After that hiatus, pain developed, tests were run, and soon I began a series of chemotherapy treatments which extended over nine months. My cancer had developed and morphed into another form, which, unchecked, would have killed me within six months to a year. I had just turned seventy-three years old.

The pain quickly became debilitating. I started on a daily cocktail of morphine and oxycodone. Nausea set in, and constipation. I began to lose weight rapidly. There were few foods I could keep down. Chemotherapy, at first one day every three weeks, was tolerable at the onset, but gradually my strength diminished. Fatigue became chronic; any activity drained my energy quickly. I was always sleepy. I was always cold. Decision-making was almost impossible, and as I subsequently realized, my decisions were often wrong-minded.

During World War 1, wounded British soldiers often called the ward nurses their angels, and it was at this period in my life that my wife became my angel. Upon her devolved all of the activities I could no longer perform for myself. She continued her daily household chores and took mine upon her shoulders. She did our driving, shopping, yard work—the myriad of details which make up our daily lives. We had to sell our home and move to a condominium; she did the planning, the packing, the cleaning, the scheduling of interim quarters during our transition from our home of almost thirty years, to our new residence.

The strength I had always admired now magnified itself, and without her firm hand and guidance, I would not have survived. I was hospitalized on an emergency basis, and it was soon discovered that my physicians were not treating the correct form of cancer. My wife led the way to force new rounds of tests. She pressed and soon had me scheduled at the Dana-Faber Institute in Boston, one of the premier cancer treatment centers in the world. A new and more intensive round of chemotherapy, called stem cell transplant and ultimately involving three weeks in isolation in the hospital, was inaugurated. I was, before and after this process, on a regimen of multiple medications daily. My wife kept these up to date, ordering refills, filling pillboxes, checking to make sure I took the proper medications at the proper intervals. My fatigue had worsened. Days and weeks passed with little activity on my part. I lost all of my hair. I was always cold—I had to wear hats even while indoors.

I was fortunate—I became a cancer survivor. Gradually my strength recovered; the chronic fatigue began to ebb. And then I was able to reflect upon what my caregiver, my wife, my angel, had given me. From the first, I knew what she gave me physically, but now I understood the emotional toll she had paid. For so long, I was a receiver and unable to give; for so long she had to struggle through her fears alone, to receive only occasional consolation and rarely any relief. I cannot tell her story nor do I need to; she has expressed herself eloquently in these pages. But I can take this moment to say thank you and to say that as I look back and consider all that was given, I know that caregiving is a great act of love. In my case, it was also a gift of life. It could have been otherwise, but nothing could ever diminish the love I was so fortunate to receive.

To the readers who are caregivers, I hope you find whatever it is that fills and refills your spirit as you provide support and care.

TESTIMONIALS

This memoir is a profoundly moving story of Helen's journey as a caregiver for her husband, who is battling cancer. The reader travels with her during the ups and downs that she faces during diagnosis, treatment, and other roadblocks along the way. Eventually Helen finds support in unlikely places and also discovers that she is much stronger than her fears. She is a survivor. (Lynn Everling, friend of author)

A caregiver's story, the story of caring for a loved one with cancer. For friends, as well as medical practitioners, we are more than an aggregation of healthy cells versus cancer cells. (Betty Trembly, friend of author)

ACKNOWLEDGMENTS

This memoir would never have happened had it not been for my editor, Laurie Edwards, and her steadfast guidance. I want to thank Dr. Eric Jacobsen, MD, for his assistance in correct medical terminology and his encouragement. Also many thanks to Dr. Nancy Skehan, MD, for her thoughtful comments that I have used throughout the book. To my daughters, Jean Avery and Lynne Everling, I thank them beyond words for their love and concern. They carried me through the roughest of days. To all who read the manuscript and offered feedback, I am indebted. Thank you, Ginni Corbin, Shirley and Bruce Avery, Lynn Everling, Russell Jewell, Judi and Bill Shipman, John Shipman, Leslie Pferchy. Special thanks to Betty Trembly for her friendship, playing taps, and her constant encouragement. To Alex Avery, my sincere thanks for showing me the rewards of perseverance and grit. I am grateful to Dan Gilmore for his detailed notes and encouragement. Many thanks to Joyce Gilmore for her insightful comments that precede some chapters—so appreciated.

ENDNOTES

1 B. Joyce Gilmore, RN (Retd.), email message to author, September 2020.
2 Ivan Turgenev Quotes, Brainyquote.com, 2021, https//www.brainyquote.com/quotes/ivan_turgenev_127435, accessed February 16, 2021.
3 John Bartlett, *Bartlett's Familiar Quotations*, 5th and 125th anniversary ed. (Little, Brown and Company, 1980), 565.
4 https://www.azquotes.com/author/19268-Harun Yahya.
5 www.goodreads.com/quotes/tag/medicine/THE MAXIMS OF MEDICI.
6 *Napoleon Hill's Positive Action Plan: 365 Meditations for Making Each Day a Success* (Penguin, 1997), 70, AZQuotes.com/Napoleon Hill.
7 bing.com/Best Quotes on Urgency/Buddha/The Trouble is.
8 Dr. Nancy T. Skehan, author's primary care physician, email message to author, September 2020.
9 "Caring for a Loved One with Cancer and Yourself," American Cancer Society, no. 0045.67.
10 Dr. Nancy T. Skehan, email message to author, September 2020.
11 https://www.goodreads.com/quotes/93512-you-may-encounter-many-defeats-but-you-must-not-be.
12 "Stem Cell Transplantation: An Information Guide for Patients and Caregivers," Dana-Farber/Brigham and Women's Cancer Center (Summer 2013), 4.
13 https://kuote/kwize.com/quote/2415.
14 B. J. Gilmore (Retd. RN), in discussion with author, October 2020.
15 Dr. Nancy T. Skehan, email message to author, September 2020.
16 https://www.goodreads.com/quotes/18064-kind-words-can-be-short-and-easy-to-speak-but.
17 Dr. Nancy T. Skehan, email message to author, September 2020.
18 *Marley & Me: Life and Love with the World's Worst Dog*, https://www.goodreads.com/quotes/john_grogan
19 "Caring for a Loved One With Cancer and Yourself," *American Cancer Society*, 5.
20 https://www.goodreads.com/quotes/tag;dogs-and humans/The bond with a dog.

ABOUT THE AUTHOR

Helen Bartucca is a graduate of Clark University and lives in Massachusetts with her husband. This is her first memoir.

CPSIA information can be obtained
at www.ICGtesting.com
Printed in the USA
JSHW081405140323
38730JS00006B/67